I0413478

Simulated Changes in Salinity in the York and Chickahominy Rivers from Projected Sea-Level Rise in Chesapeake Bay

By Karen C. Rice, Mark R. Bennett, and Jian Shen

Prepared in cooperation with the City of Newport News

Open-File Report 2011–1191

U.S. Department of the Interior
U.S. Geological Survey

U.S. Department of the Interior
KEN SALAZAR, Secretary

U.S. Geological Survey
Marcia K. McNutt, Director

U.S. Geological Survey, Reston, Virginia: 2011

For more information on the USGS—the Federal source for science about the Earth, its natural and living resources, natural hazards, and the environment, visit http://www.usgs.gov or call 1-888-ASK-USGS

For an overview of USGS information products, including maps, imagery, and publications,
visit http://www.usgs.gov/pubprod

To order this and other USGS information products, visit http://store.usgs.gov

Any use of trade, product, or firm names is for descriptive purposes only and does not imply endorsement by the U.S. Government.

Although this report is in the public domain, permission must be secured from the individual copyright owners to reproduce any copyrighted materials contained within this report.

Suggested citation:
Rice, K.C., Bennett, M.R., and Shen, Jian, 2011, Simulated changes in salinity in the York and Chickahominy Rivers from projected sea-level rise in Chesapeake Bay: U.S. Geological Survey Open-File Report 2011–1191, 31 p.

Contents

Figures

Tables

Conversion Factors

SI to Inch/Pound

Multiply	By	To obtain
Length		
centimeter (cm)	0.3937	inch (in.)
millimeter (mm)	0.03937	inch (in.)
millimeter per year (mm/yr)	0.03937	inch per year (in/yr)
meter (m)	3.281	foot (ft)
kilometer (km)	0.6214	mile (mi)
kilometer (km)	0.5400	mile, nautical (nmi)
meter (m)	1.094	yard (yd)
Area		
square kilometer (km^2)	0.6214	square mile (mi^2)
Volume		
liter (L)	0.2642	gallon (gal)
cubic meter per second (m^3/s)	264.2	gallon (gal)
cubic meter (m^3)	0.0002642	million gallons (Mgal)
Flow rate		
cubic meter per second (m^3/s)	35.31	cubic foot per second (ft^3/s)

Temperature in degrees Fahrenheit (°F) may be converted to degrees Celsius (°C) as follows:

$$°C = (°F-32)/1.8$$

Acronyms and Additional Abbreviations

TDS	Total dissolved solids
GMSL	Global mean sea level
IPCC	Intergovernmental Panel on Climate Change
mg/L	Milligrams per liter
ppt	Parts per thousand
river km	River kilometer
HEM-3D	Three-Dimensional Hydrodynamic-Eutrophication Model
DEQ	Virginia Department of Environmental Quality
VIMS	Virginia Institute of Marine Science
NOAA	National Oceanic and Atmospheric Administration

Simulated Changes in Salinity in the York and Chickahominy Rivers from Projected Sea-Level Rise in Chesapeake Bay

By Karen C. Rice[1], Mark R. Bennett[1], and Jian Shen[2]

Abstract

As a result of climate change and variability, sea level is rising throughout the world, but the rate along the east coast of the United States is higher than the global mean rate. The U.S. Geological Survey, in cooperation with the City of Newport News, Virginia, conducted a study to evaluate the effects of possible future sea-level rise on the salinity front in two tributaries to Chesapeake Bay, the York River, and the Chickahominy/James River estuaries. Numerical modeling was used to represent sea-level rise and the resulting hydrologic effects. Estuarine models for the two tributaries were developed and model simulations were made by use of the Three-Dimensional Hydrodynamic-Eutrophication Model (HEM-3D), developed by the Virginia Institute of Marine Science. HEM-3D was used to simulate tides, tidal currents, and salinity for Chesapeake Bay, the York River and the Chickahominy/James River. The three sea-level rise scenarios that were evaluated showed an increase of 30, 50, and 100 centimeters (cm).

Model results for both estuaries indicated that high freshwater river flow was effective in pushing the salinity back toward Chesapeake Bay. Model results indicated that increases in mean salinity will greatly alter the existing water-quality gradients between brackish water and freshwater. This will be particularly important for the freshwater part of the Chickahominy River, where a drinking-water-supply intake for the City of Newport News is located.

Significant changes in the salinity gradients for the York River and Chickahominy/James River estuaries were predicted for the three sea-level rise scenarios. When a 50-cm sea-level rise scenario on the York River during a typical year (2005) was used, the model simulation showed a salinity of 15 parts per thousand (ppt) at river kilometer (km) 39. During a dry year (2002), the same salinity (15 ppt) was simulated at river km 45, which means that saltwater was shown to migrate 6 km farther upstream during a dry year than a typical year.

The same was true of the Chickahominy River for a 50-cm sea-level rise scenario but to a greater extent; a salinity of 4 ppt was simulated at river km 13 during a typical year and at river km 28 during a dry year, indicating that saltwater migrated 15 km farther upstream during a dry year.

Near a drinking-water intake on the Chickahominy River, for a dry year, salinity is predicted to more than double for all three sea-level rise scenarios, relative to a typical year. During a typical year at this location, salinity is predicted to increase to 0.006, 0.07, and more than 2 ppt for the 30-, 50-, and 100-cm rise scenarios, respectively.

Introduction

Society faces many environmental problems and challenges, but the recent threat of climate change and variability has become a prominent focus for both government and industry. Some of the consequences of climate change and variability are water availability for municipal and industrial use, water demand for irrigation, changes in water quality, threats to stormwater and wastewater infrastructure, and changes in sea level. An Intergovernmental Panel on Climate Change (IPCC) assessment report concludes, "Observational records and climate projections provide abundant evidence that freshwater resources are vulnerable and have the potential to be strongly impacted by climate change, with wide-ranging consequences for human societies and ecosystems" (Bates and others, 2008).

The purpose of this study was to utilize a hydrodynamic simulation model to evaluate possible future changes in salinity in the York River and Chickahominy/James River estuaries resulting from projected sea-level rise. The scope of this report is to describe the models used and present the results of the model simulations for the York and Chickahominy/James Rivers.

The regional distribution of salinity in the York River and Chickahominy/James River estuaries from projected sea-level rise is a critical element needed by water managers and others

[1] U.S. Geological Survey, Virginia Water Science Center, Richmond, Va.

[2] Department of Physical Sciences, Virginia Institute of Marine Science, Gloucester Point, Va.

concerned with protecting the Chesapeake Bay and its estuaries. In 2009, the U.S. Geological Survey (USGS), in cooperation with the City of Newport News, Virginia (Va.), began a study to investigate the potential effects of future sea-level rise on salinity change in two estuaries in southeastern Virginia. The two estuaries, the York River and the Chickahominy/James River, discharge into Chesapeake Bay. This report provides information about the sea-level rise study and the results of model simulations of changes in salinity.

Climate Variability and Change and Sea-Level Rise

Earth has a long history of climate variability and change, which includes periods of cooling and warming, and sea-level rise. Earth's historical surface-temperature variations, derived from a variety of sources, show that there has been a warming trend since the early 1800s (fig. 1). A recent ice core collected from the Vostok site in Antarctica extends our knowledge of Earth's climate to 420,000 years before present. According to data from the Vostok ice core, temperature has varied about 12 degrees Celsius (°C) in fairly regular ±100,000-year cycles over this much longer record (Petit and others, 2000). Warmer air temperature leads to many environmental changes, including warmer ocean water, an increase in tropical storm intensity, sea-level rise, ocean and coastal changes, and changes in precipitation patterns.

Like the fluctuations in Earth's climate, sea level also has fluctuated over the past 400,000 years (fig. 2). Evidence suggests that sea level was about 4 to 6 meters (m) higher than present during the last interglacial warm period 125,000 years ago and 120 m lower during the last Ice Age, about 21,000 years ago (see reviews in Muhs and others, 2004, and Overpeck and others, 2006). More recently, during the current warming period, global mean sea level (GMSL) has risen about 0.25 m since measuring commenced in 1870 and is projected to rise an additional 0.5 m by the year 2100 (fig. 3).

Specific environmental effects of future global climate variability and change remain uncertain; in particular, there is large uncertainty in whether the changes will occur gradually or abruptly. A certainty, however, is that as air temperature rises, polar ice caps and glaciers melt, and sea level rises from the influx of melt water. Increased air and water temperature will cause thermal expansion of the oceans, which also will contribute to sea-level rise.

Sea-level rise can affect coastal and estuarine areas in several ways, including causing increased shoreline erosion, inundation of low-lying coastal areas, increased damage from storms and flooding, changes in the existence and distribution of wetlands and associated biota, and encroachment of saline water into estuaries and coastal aquifers. If estuarine salinity were to move far enough upstream into freshwater rivers, it is likely to affect municipal drinking-water supplies, as well as alter habitat for plant and animal communities.

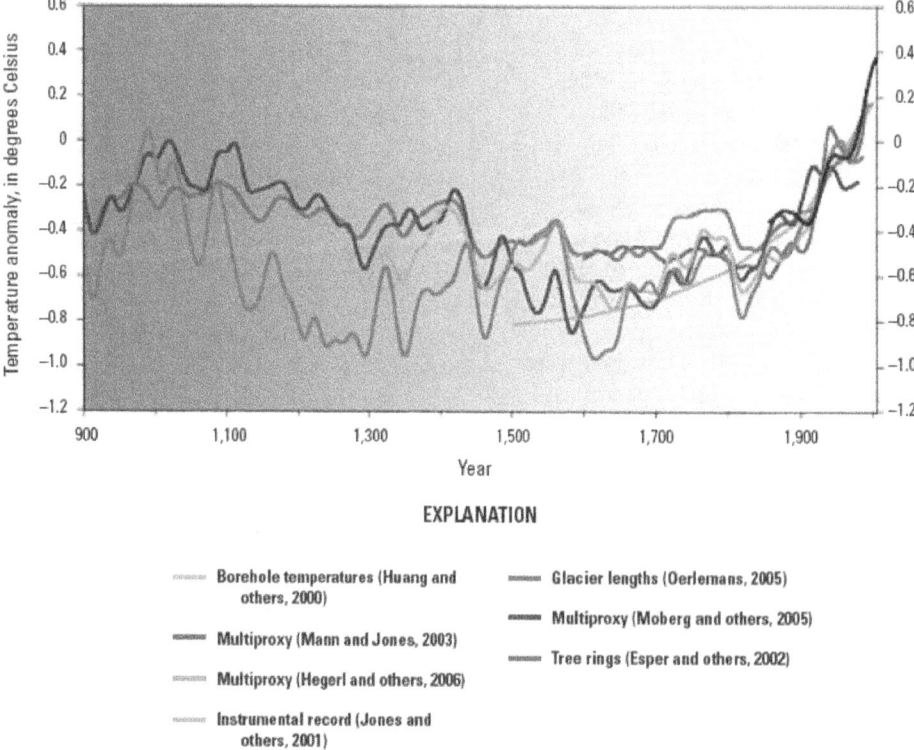

EXPLANATION

.... Borehole temperatures (Huang and others, 2000)

——— Multiproxy (Mann and Jones, 2003)

········ Multiproxy (Hegerl and others, 2006)

········ Instrumental record (Jones and others, 2001)

——— Glacier lengths (Oerlemans, 2005)

——— Multiproxy (Moberg and others, 2005)

——— Tree rings (Esper and others, 2002)

Figure 1. Smoothed reconstructions of large-scale surface temperature variations (Northern Hemisphere mean or global mean) from proxy records and the instrumental record (beginning in 1856) of global mean surface temperature. Darker gray shading indicates greater generalized uncertainty (National Research Council, 2006).

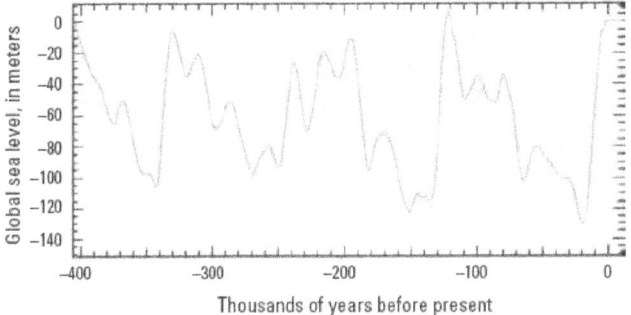

Figure 2. Variations in global sea-level elevation over the last 400,000 years resulting from four natural glacial and interglacial cycles. Reprinted from Quaternary Science Reviews (Huybrechts, 2002).

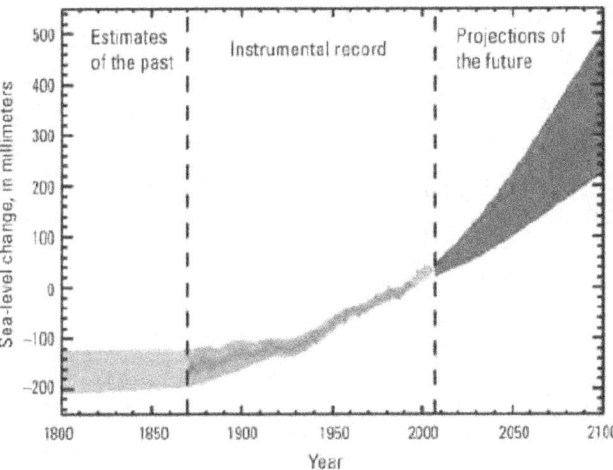

Figure 3. Past and projected global average sea level. The gray shaded area shows the estimates of sea-level change from 1800 to 1870 when measurements were not available. The red line is a reconstruction of sea-level change measured by tidal gages with the surrounding shaded area depicting the uncertainty. The green line shows sea-level change as measured by satellite. The purple shaded area represents the range of Global Circulation Model projections for a medium-growth emissions scenario (Intergovernmental Panel on Climate Change SRES A1B). For reference, 100 millimeters is about 4 inches. From Intergovernmental Panel on Climate Change (2007).

As climate patterns continue to change, natural variability also will continue. Any projected change in average river runoff, air temperature, and sea level will occur in addition to ongoing natural variability. In many cases, the amplitude of the natural variability can be quite large compared to the changes projected to result from global warming (Miller and Yates, 2006). Furthermore, relatively short instrumental records may not provide an adequate picture of the full range of natural climate variability. The longer-term view provided by geologic evidence, such as ice-core data, and recent climate research based on tree rings, are crucial when evaluating change and the rates of change (for example, fig. 1).

Drinking-Water Utilities and Climate Change

Surface-temperature variations and sea-level rise have implications for water-resources management. The engineering and economic approaches that underlie virtually all historical water planning in the United States, however, assume that climatic and hydrologic processes are nearly stationary. Effective management of existing water-resources infrastructure depends on adaption to current realities, including physical condition of infrastructure, competing demands, public values, population, and climate, none that are static. Establishing a reasonable range for variability will be a key element and challenge for water-supply management.

Personnel at public drinking-water utilities have spent most of the past decade identifying the specific water-quality and quantity changes that likely will be experienced, and the changes or threshold-level events that may be experienced, as a result of global change. Sustainability, resilience, and adaptability have emerged and coalesced as both goals and solutions for the drinking-water sector. To adequately simulate the effect that climate change could have on a specific region, a model must be scaled down from those used on a global scale.

The technical term for the degree of saltiness of surface waters is "salinity." Water is considered to be fresh when salinity is less than 500 milligrams per liter (mg/L) total dissolved solids (TDS); 500 mg/L is equivalent to 0.5 parts per thousand (ppt, the salinity unit used in this report). The U.S. Environmental Protection Agency's secondary standard for drinking water for TDS is 500 mg/L (*http://water.epa.gov/drink/contaminants/index.cfm*; accessed 7/21/2011). When salinity is between 0.5 and 30 ppt, water is considered to be brackish.

Newport News Waterworks is a regional drinking-water utility located on the Virginia Lower Peninsula, which is bounded on the north and south by the brackish tidal estuaries of the York and James Rivers, respectively (fig. 4). Newport News Waterworks serves about 415,000 people, including eight Federal installations. The water-treatment facilities for this sector and a growing multijurisdictional service area are located on the Virginia Lower Peninsula.

A Newport News Waterworks public water-supply intake is located in a lake upstream of Walkers Dam, a tidal-barrier dam on the Chickahominy River estuary (fig. 4). The quantity and quality of water available for utility withdrawal from this location are dependent on climate variability, which can cause changes in river flow, lake stage, and salinity levels. About 30 to 70 percent of the region's drinking-water supply originates as transfers from the lake at Walkers Dam. When inflow to the various supply reservoirs is severely diminished during droughts, withdrawals from the lake at Walkers Dam are crucial. A consequence of reduced freshwater flows during droughts is increased salinity levels in the estuary. Historical water-quality data confirm that when freshwater flow is diminished in the James and Chickahominy Rivers, saline water moves upstream to Walkers Dam (Ron Harris, Newport News Waterworks, written commun., 2010). Therefore, any increase

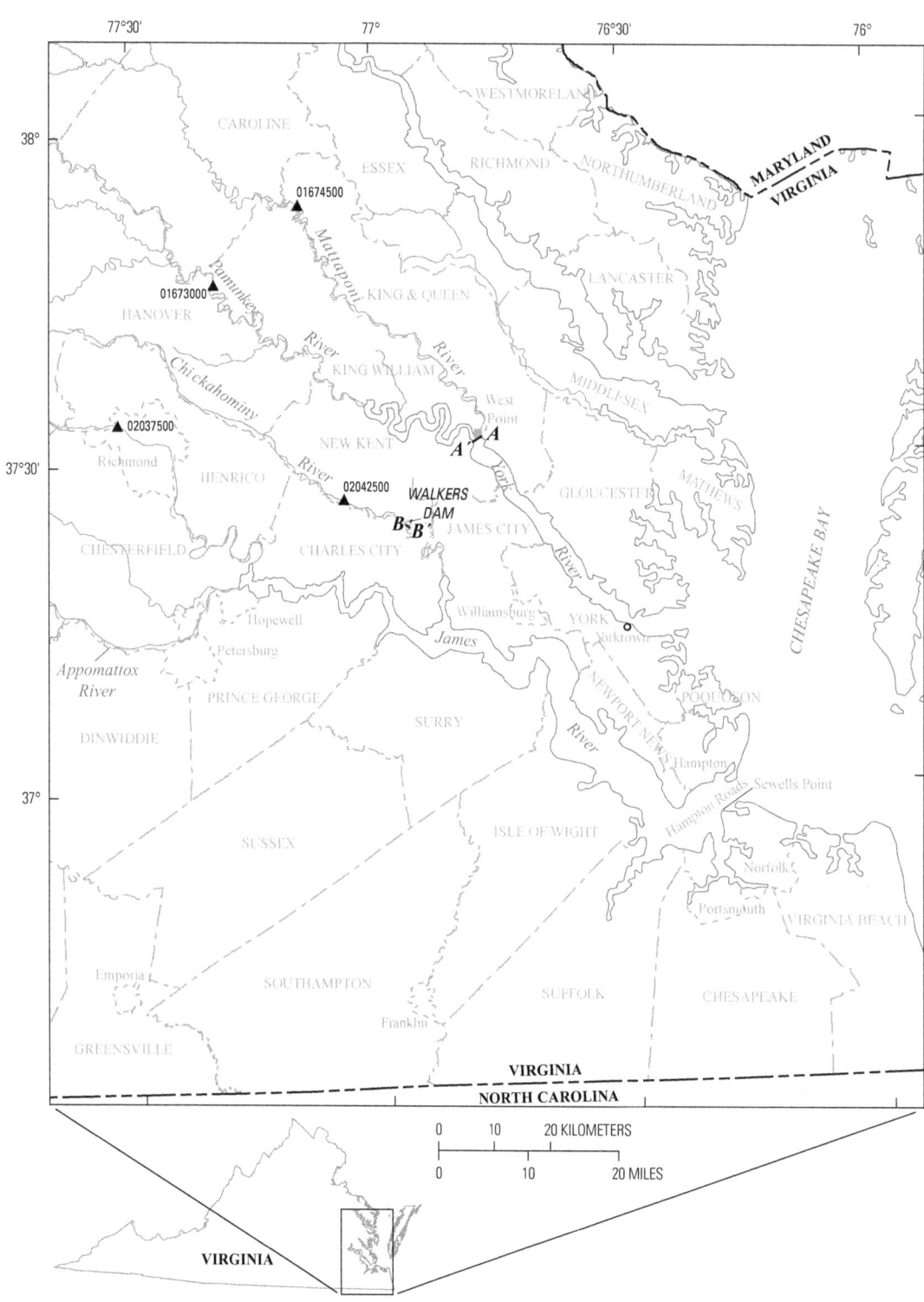

Figure 4. Location of York, Chickahominy, and James Rivers, Virginia.

in the occurrence or duration of salinity at the location of the intake could affect the safe yield and sustainability of the surface-water system.

In addition to the effects of reduced freshwater flows on water quality, utilities need to be aware of the effects of potential sea-level rise on water quality. In general, sea-level rise can cause saline water to migrate upstream to points where freshwater existed previously (National Research Council, 1987; Poff and others, 2002; Climate Change Science Program, 2009). A salinity migration may cause loss of salt-sensitive habitat that would affect surface-water and groundwater drinking-water supplies, as well as habitat loss for a variety of plants and animals.

One way to assess potential future changes in environmental systems is to develop accurate science-based models of present-day environmental system behavior. Once present-day processes can be simulated, the models can be used to investigate a plausible range of future changes. Changes in environmental processes typically are interrelated with each other and a variety of other factors, resulting in complex feedback loops.

Study Area

The study area includes two tributaries to Chesapeake Bay, the York River and the Chickahominy/James River (fig. 4). The York River is the fifth largest tributary basin that discharges to Chesapeake Bay and is formed at West Point, Va., by the confluence of the Mattaponi and Pamunkey Rivers. The York River flows southeastward and discharges to the bay between the York-James and Middle Peninsulas of Virginia. The Chickahominy River is located south of West Point and flows southward to join the James River, which flows southeastward and discharges to the bay south of the Lower Peninsula.

Sea-Level Rise in Chesapeake Bay

Global mean sea level has risen 10 to 15 cm over the last 100 years (Ayers and others, 1994) and the rate from 1993 to 2003 has been reported at 3.1 millimeters per year (mm/yr; Intergovernmental Panel on Climate Change, 2007). The measured rate of rise along the east coast of the United States (table 1) relative to land surface has been greater than the GMSL rise because of local land subsidence (Hull and Titus, 1986).

Relative sea-level rise refers to the change in sea level relative to the elevation of the adjacent land, which can also subside or rise as a result of natural and human-induced factors. Relative sea-level changes include both global sea-level rise and changes in the vertical elevation of the land surface. Land surface of southeastern Virginia is sinking because of isostatic rebound to the north from the most recent glaciation. In addition, land subsidence from groundwater withdrawal in southeastern Virginia has been documented (Pope and Burbey, 2004). In this report, "sea-level rise" refers to relative sea-level rise.

Table 1. Rates of relative sea-level rise for selected long-term tidal gages on the Atlantic coast of the United States.

[For comparison, the global average rate of sea-level rise is 1.7 millimeters per year (mm/yr; from Williams and others, 2009); ±, plus or minus]

Station	Rate of sea-level rise (mm/yr)	Time span of record
Eastport, Maine	2.12 ± 0.13	1929–1999
Portland, Maine	1.91 ± 0.09	1912–1999
Seavey Island, Maine	1.75 ± 0.17	1926–1999
Boston, Massachusetts	2.65 ± 0.10	1921–1999
Woods Hole, Massachusetts	2.59 ± 0.12	1932–1999
Providence, Rhode Island	1.88 ± 0.17	1938–1999
Newport, Rhode Island	2.57 ± 0.11	1930–1999
New London, Connecticut	2.13 ± 0.15	1938–1999
Montauk, New York	2.58 ± 0.19	1947–1999
Willets Point, New York	2.41 ± 0.15	1931–1999
The Battery, New York	2.77 ± 0.05	1905–1999
Sandy Hook, New Jersey	3.88 ± 0.15	1932–1999
Atlantic City, New Jersey	3.98 ± 0.11	1911–1999
Philadelphia, Pennsylvania	2.75 ± 0.12	1900–1999
Lewes, Delaware	3.16 ± 0.16	1919–1999
Baltimore, Maryland	3.12 ± 0.08	1902–1999
Annapolis, Maryland	3.53 ± 0.13	1928–1999
Solomons Island, Maryland	3.29 ± 0.17	1937–1999
Washington, D.C.	3.13 ± 0.21	1931–1999
Hampton Roads, Virginia	4.42 ± 0.16	1927–1999
Portsmouth, Virginia	3.76 ± 0.23	1935–1999
Wilmington, North Carolina	2.22 ± 0.25	1935–1999
Charleston, South Carolina	3.28 ± 0.14	1921–1999
Fort Pulaski, Georgia	3.05 ± 0.20	1935–1999
Fernandina Beach, Florida	2.04 ± 0.12	1897–1999
Mayport, Florida	2.43 ± 0.18	1928–1999
Miami, Florida	2.39 ± 0.22	1931–1999
Key West, Florida	2.27 ± 0.09	1913–1999

In the mid-to-upper Chesapeake Bay region, local sea-level rise averages between 3.1 and 3.5 mm/yr. Farther south in the lower Chesapeake Bay region, local sea-level rise is higher, averaging 3.6 to 7.0 mm/yr (Boon and others, 2008). The highest rate of sea-level rise for the east coast, 4.42 mm/yr, is reported for Hampton Roads, Va. (table 1). At Sewells Point, Va., a tidal gage indicates that average sea level has risen at a rate of about 4.44 mm/yr from 1927 through 2006 (fig. 5).

The magnitude of the effects of climate change and variability in Chesapeake Bay will be influenced in large part through changes of physical processes, such as precipitation, wind, tides, and freshwater river discharge to the bay. The

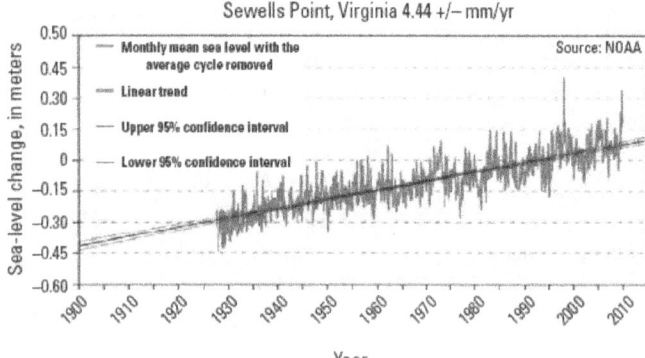

Figure 5. Historic sea-level rise at Sewells Point, Virginia, 1927–2006 (National Oceanic and Atmospheric Administration, 2010).

physical processes will mediate change through dynamics that amplify or suppress rates and magnitudes of change. A recent article by Najjar and others (2010) reviews the potential effect of climate change on Chesapeake Bay. On the basis of current understanding, they find that: (1) sea level will rise 0.7 to 1.6 m by the end of the 21st century; (2) precipitation amount is likely to increase in the winter and spring; (3) precipitation intensity is likely to increase; and (4) droughts are likely to increase in both frequency and duration. The Hampton Roads Planning District Commission confirms that climate change could affect water resources significantly in the region (MacFarlane and Walberg, 2010).

Estuaries are vertically stratified, with denser more saline water lying below less dense and less saline water. Because of interactions of tides and freshwater inflow, this difference in density produces a two-layered flow situation, a common characteristic of estuaries. The denser saline bottom water enters the estuary from Chesapeake Bay and flows upstream, whereas the less dense surface waters, dominated by freshwater discharge, flow downstream toward the bay. Salinity variations throughout Chesapeake Bay have been shown to be strongly tied to river discharge (Schubel and Pritchard, 1986). In turn, Chesapeake Bay estuaries exhibit large seasonal variations in salinity (represented by chloride concentration in fig. 6).

Simple models are able to accurately predict monthly average salinity throughout the mainstem of the bay from the flow of the Susquehanna River (Gibson and Najjar, 2000). A clear signal of salinity change in Chesapeake Bay from sea-level rise was detected by Hilton and others (2008), and a recent study indicates that salinity in the bay has the potential to increase by 2 ppt (Najjar and others, 2010). No detailed studies of potential effects of salinity-front migration as a result of sea-level rise have been performed on any tributaries that discharge to the bay. When and where the saline water displaces the freshwater is of great interest to a wide variety of stakeholders.

Salinity variability in Chesapeake Bay estuaries is monitored by a number of organizations, including the Virginia Department of Environmental Quality (DEQ), the Virginia

Institute of Marine Science (VIMS), the City of Newport News, and the Chesapeake Bay Program. DEQ has been collecting specific conductance and salinity data at multiple locations and at varying depths in the York River estuary since 1979, and VIMS has collected salinity data at 6-minute intervals at the mouth of the York River estuary since 1986. The City of Newport News has monitored specific conductance and chloride concentrations along the Chickahominy River at about 10 locations (some sites have been discontinued and others added) since 1997. The Chesapeake Bay Program (*http://www.chesapeakebay.net/*) has overseen the majority of the salinity monitoring in and around the bay since 1984.

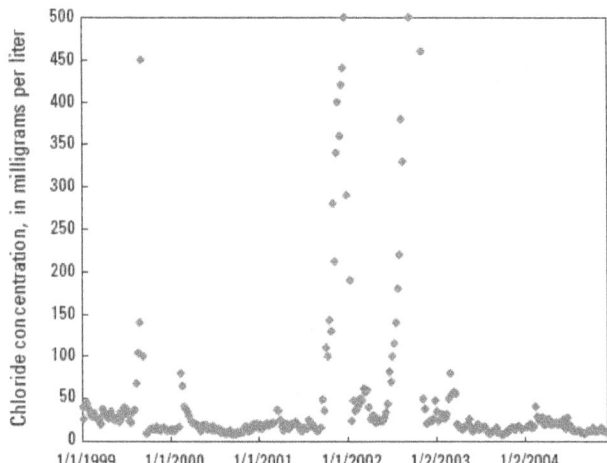

Figure 6. Chloride concentration at Walkers Dam on the Chickahominy River, 1999–2004.

Sea-Level Rise Scenarios

This report does not provide a forecast of future rates of sea-level rise. Rather, the implications of three reasonable estimates of sea-level rise scenarios over the next century were evaluated. A recent U.S. report (Climate Change Science Program, 2009) synthesized an enormous amount of climatic and oceanic modeling and proposed three sea-level rise scenarios for the 21st century for the mid-Atlantic region. The scenarios were developed from a combination of the 20th century sea-level rise rate and either a 2- or 7-mm/yr increase in global sea level, and are as follows:

- Scenario 1: The 20th century rate, which is generally 3 to 4 mm/yr in the mid-Atlantic region (30 to 40 cm total by the year 2100);

- Scenario 2: The 20th century rate plus 2 mm/yr acceleration (up to 50 cm total by 2100); and

- Scenario 3: The 20th century rate plus 7 mm/yr acceleration (up to 100 cm total by 2100).

Scenario 1 assesses the effect if future sea-level rise occurs at the same rate as was observed over the 20th century at a particular location. Scenarios 1 and 2 are within the range of those reported by IPCC (2007). Scenario 3 exceeds the IPCC scenario range by up to 40 cm by 2100. Higher estimates on the basis of possible warmer air temperature have been suggested by Chand and others (2009), although no consensus on the likely upper bound of GMSL currently exists.

The three sea-level rise scenarios bracket the current scientific research relating to mid-Atlantic sea-level rise. As such, rises of 30, 50, and 100 cm were selected for the modeling component of this study, and they are referred to as the 30-cm, 50-cm, and 100-cm scenarios, respectively. Temporal variability is an important consideration, because years with lower-than-normal river flow (drought conditions) will allow the salinity front to migrate farther upstream as sea level rises. Years with higher-than-normal river flow, however, will counteract upstream salinity movement.

Hydrodynamic Models

The Virginia Institute of Marine Science developed a numerical model for Chesapeake Bay and parts of its Virginia tributaries. The model has been applied to a wide range of environmental studies in the Chesapeake Bay system and other estuarine systems (Hamrick, 1992; Sisson and others, 1997; Shen and Haas, 2004; Shen and Lin, 2006). The simulator used to develop the Chesapeake Bay model is called the Three-Dimensional Hydrodynamic-Eutrophication Model (HEM-3D). The Environmental Fluid Dynamics Code makes up the hydrodynamic part of the HEM-3D model (Hamrick, 1992; Park and others, 1995) and resembles the widely used Blumberg Mellor model (Blumberg and Mellor, 1987) in both the physics and the computational schemes. The full hydrodynamic shallow-wave equations are solved in three dimensions. The model is capable of simulating density and topographically induced circulation; tidal and wind-driven flows; and spatial and temporal distributions of salinity, temperature, suspended-sediment concentration, and conservative tracers. The model solves the three-dimensional continuity and free-surface equations of motion. The Mellor and Yamada level 2.5 turbulence closure scheme was implemented in the model (Mellor and Yamada, 1982; Galperin and others, 1988). The model uses stretched (or sigma) vertical coordinates and Cartesian (or curvilinear) orthogonal horizontal coordinates.

The modeling done for this project built upon previously developed models of the York and James Rivers and the Chesapeake Bay. A nested-grid modeling approach was used to simulate salinity with sufficient resolution while not sacrificing computational efficiency. HEM-3D was used to simulate tides, tidal currents, and salinity for Chesapeake Bay, creating boundary conditions for the York and James Rivers. To reduce the influence of the boundary conditions on the interior model domain, a large domain model that encompasses both the Chesapeake Bay mainstem and tributaries was used to simulate salinity changes from sea-level rise in Chesapeake Bay. The model uses a high-resolution grid placed in the main channel of the bay and relatively coarse grids in the tributaries

(fig. 7). This grid configuration allows the model to simulate estuarine dynamics accurately and provide boundary conditions for high-resolution models developed for the York River and the Chickahominy/James River. The Chesapeake Bay model consists of 8,932 horizontal grids with 20 vertical layers. The period of simulation for the purpose of this study was 10 years, from 1998 through 2007.

Model Limitations

The modeling scenarios do not consider future changes in freshwater flows in the York, James, or Chickahominy Rivers. Generally, scientists estimate that the eastern United States will receive more precipitation because of climate change (Brekke and others, 2009) and that individual storms in the Chesapeake Bay area will become more intense (Najjar and others, 2010). In addition, the modeling scenarios do not consider future increases in the salinity of the ocean or at the mouth of Chesapeake Bay, both of which are expected to occur with climate change (MacFarlane and Walberg, 2010).

Because of the nested modeling approach, any errors that occur in the Chesapeake Bay model propagate to the York and Chickahominy/James Rivers. Given that there are no daily observations at the mouth of the Chesapeake Bay and that wind forcing at one station was used for both the entire York and Chickahominy/James Rivers, some discrepancies between the predicted and observed salinity occur for parts of the simulations. A sensitivity analysis of the Chickahominy River model was performed (appendix). The sensitivity analysis indicated that the model was most sensitive to a decrease in river discharge and change of salinity concentration at the open boundary. The model also is sensitive to wind and change of bottom roughness. Testing an increase in river discharge or an increase in boundary salinity, however, were some of the alternatives not attempted.

York River Model

The existing York River model (Shen and Haas, 2004), which includes the Pamunkey and Mattaponi Rivers that form the York River, was modified for this study. The model, modified by deepening the bathymetry of the river, includes 3,839 horizontal grid cells with 8 vertical layers. The grid scale ranges from 250 to 800 m in the York River and was explicitly linked to the coarse-grid tributary part of the Chesapeake Bay model (fig. 8). The hourly time-series outputs of salinity and tide (surface elevation) from the bay model near the York River mouth were used to force the York River model. The timestep used for the York River model was 30 seconds. For freshwater discharge, the upstream boundaries of the model were the USGS stream gages on the Mattaponi (USGS gage 01674500) and Pamunkey (USGS gage 01673000) Rivers. Hourly wind data at Sewells Point from 1998 to 2003, and data at Yorktown from 2004 to 2007, were used as wind forcing (fig. 4). Monthly salinity data used for model calibration were obtained from the Chesapeake Bay Program.

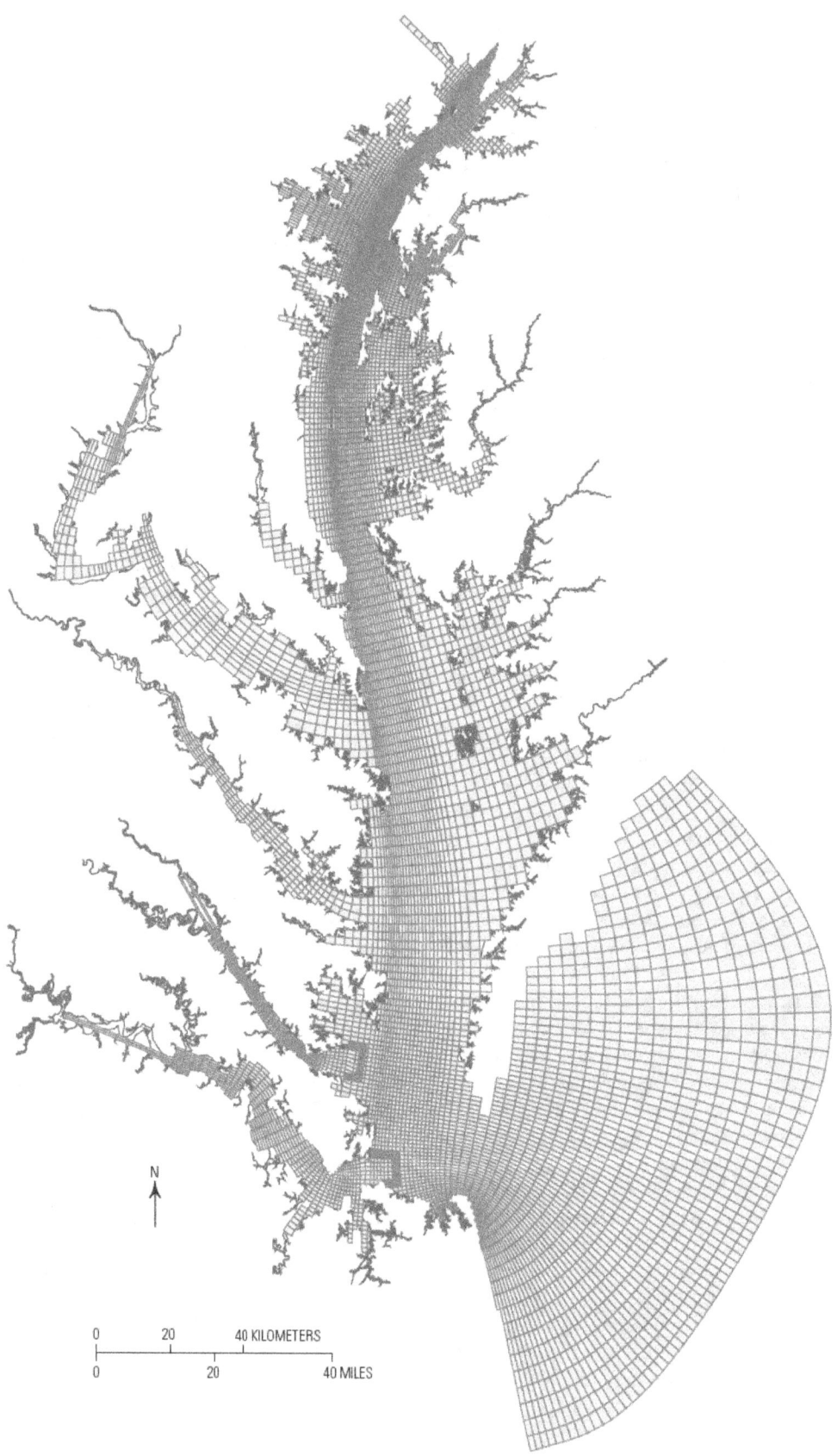

Figure 7.   Large domain model of Chesapeake Bay. The locations of the linkages of the Chesapeake Bay model with the York River and James River models are denoted by the bold red line at the mouth of each river.

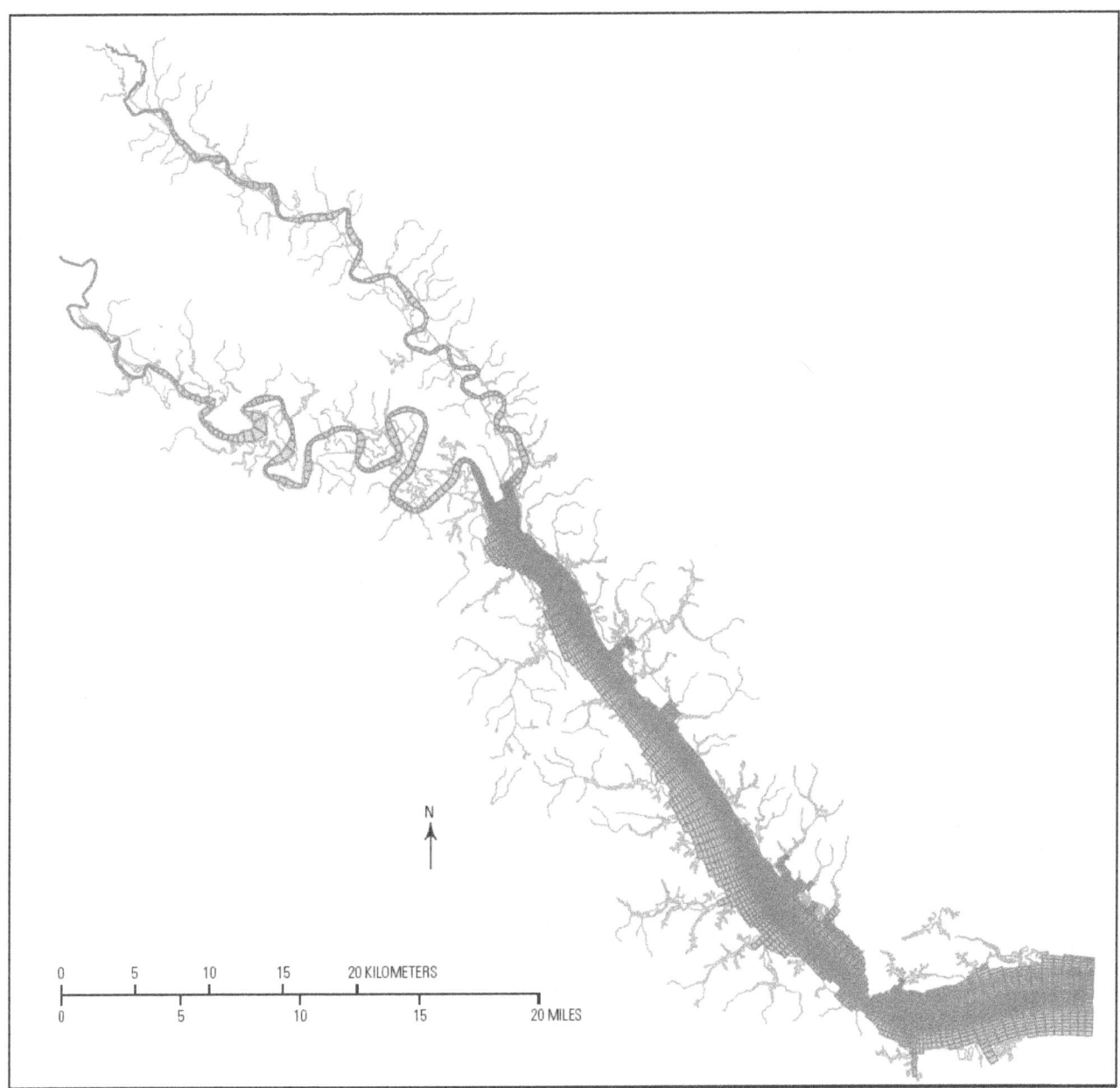

Figure 8.   Nested-grid model of the York River.

Chickahominy River Model

The existing model for the James River consists of a high-resolution model grid with 4,715 horizontal grid cells and 8 vertical layers (Shen and others, 1999; Shen and Lin, 2006). The Chickahominy River model was developed for this study with 1,158 horizontal grids and 8 vertical layers (fig. 9). The James River model was explicitly linked to the Chickahominy River model. The resulting Chickahominy/James River model was forced by the outputs of tide and salinity from the Chesapeake Bay model. The time step for the Chickahominy/ James River model was 20 seconds. For freshwater discharge, the upstream boundaries of the model were the USGS stream gages on the James (USGS gage 02037500), Appomattox

(USGS gage 02040000), and Chickahominy (USGS gage 02042500) Rivers. Hourly wind data at Sewells Point from 1998 to 2003 and data at Yorktown from 2004 to 2007 were used as wind forcing (fig. 4).

Model Results

Results of the model simulations are shown for a no-rise scenario and the three sea-level rise scenarios. Results are presented relative to a "typical" year for river discharge in southeastern Virginia. The discharge record for the James River near Richmond (USGS gage 02037500) for calendar years 1990 through 2009 was used to determine a "typical" year, a

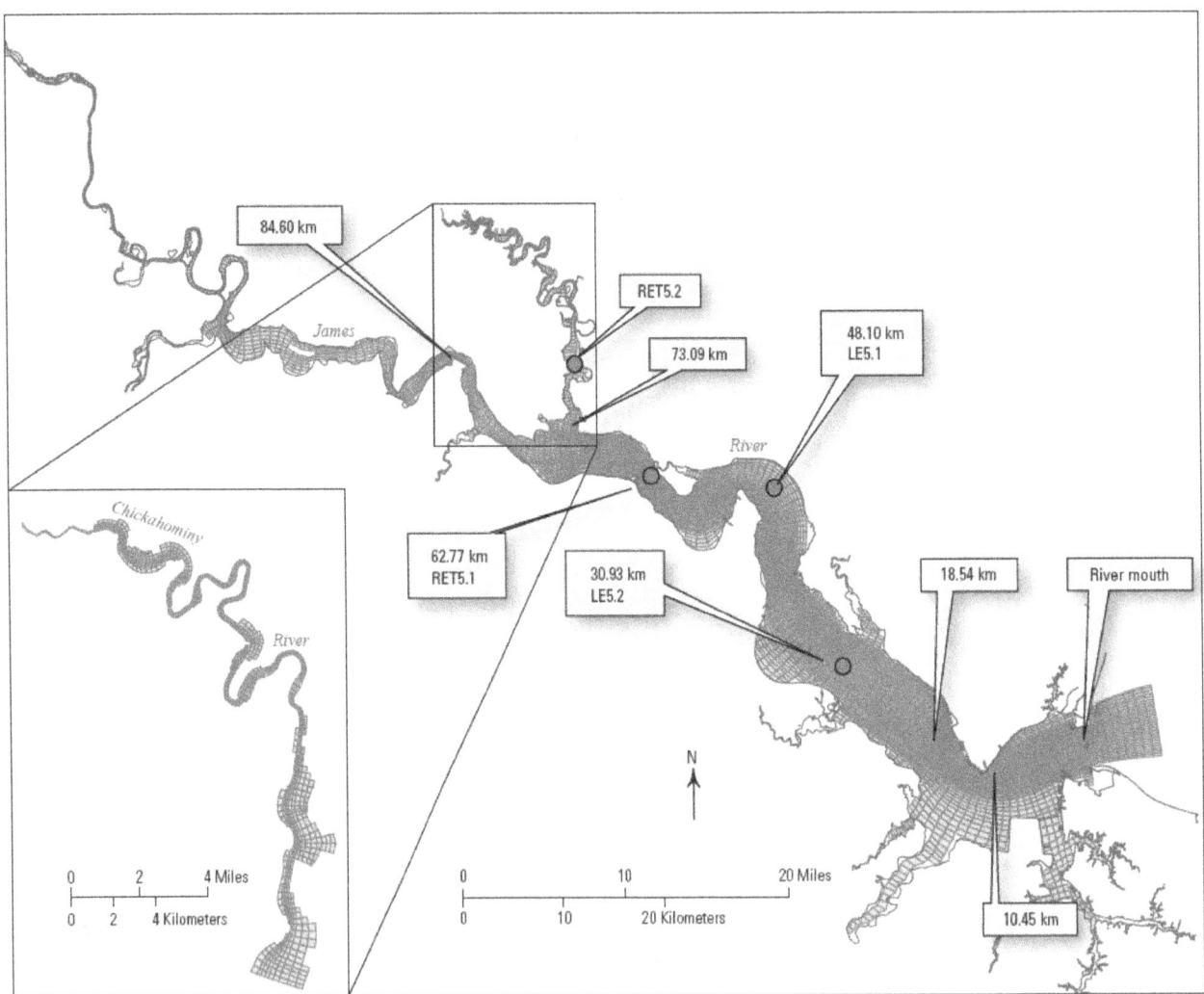

Figure 9. Nested-grid model of the James and Chickahominy Rivers. The location of the linkage of the James River and Chickahominy River models is denoted by the bold red line at the mouth of the Chickahominy River.

"wet" year, and a "dry" year. The annual mean discharge for this time interval indicated that a typical year was 2005, a wet year was 2003, and a dry year was 2002 (table 2).

York River

Results from the York River simulations are presented for the location at the confluence of the Mattaponi and Pamunkey Rivers (fig. 4), referred to as the "head of the York estuary." At this location, data were recorded showing the number of days from June 1 through December 31 that salinity was predicted to exceed 0.1 ppt (100 mg/L TDS). This 7-month (214-day) period was chosen, because river flow in the southeastern Virginia region tends to decline during the second half of the calendar year. This decline allows the model to simulate a "worst-case scenario" with respect to saltwater migration into the estuary. During both a typical and a dry year at this location, salinity is expected to exceed 0.1 ppt on each of the 214

days (table 3). In contrast, during a wet year when river flow is higher, 0.1 ppt of salinity is simulated as being reached a fewer number of days for the no-rise scenario (183 days) and the 30- and 50-cm rise scenarios (201 and 211 days, respectively), but simulated to exceed 0.1 ppt for all of the 214 days for the 100-cm rise scenario (table 3).

The 10-year time-series simulated salinity data from the no-rise scenario and the three sea-level rise scenarios indicated that salinity is highest during a dry year (2002) and that salinity is projected to increase as sea level rises, at the surface of the water as well as at depth (fig. 10). In contrast, a wet year (2003) decreases the salinity substantially (fig. 10).

Cross sections of average salinity simulated at the head of the York estuary are shown for July and August (fig. 11), September and October (fig. 12), and November and December (fig. 13); the scale for salinity is not uniform for all panels in these figures. The cross section (A–A') is viewed looking downstream (the left side of the section is the northeast side of the river).

Table 2. Mean annual discharge for the James River near Richmond (for calendar years 1990 through 2009).

[USGS gage 02037500; records provided by Virginia Department of Environmental Quality, Water Division. m³/s, cubic meters per second; shaded dates are the years for which results are reported]

Chronological order		Lowest-to-highest order	
Year	Mean annual discharge, m³/s	Year	Mean annual discharge, m³/s
1990	231	2002	102
1991	190	2001	103
1992	197	2008	116
1993	251	1999	124
1994	233	2000	133
1995	197	2007	161
1996	321	1997	181
1997	181	1991	190
1998	307	2006	191
1999	124	2005	194
2000	133	1992	197
2001	103	1995	197
2002	102	2009	204
2003	414	1990	231
2004	269	1994	233
2005	194	1993	251
2006	191	2004	269
2007	161	1998	307
2008	116	1996	321
2009	204	2003	414

Table 3. Number of days that salinity is predicted to exceed 0.1 parts per thousand at the head of the York estuary from June 1 to December 31 (total 214 days) of the year indicated for the no-rise scenario and the three sea-level rise scenarios.

[cm, centimeter]

Model scenario	Dry year 2002	Wet year 2003	Typical year 2005
No rise	214	183	214
30-cm rise	214	201	214
50-cm rise	214	211	214
100-cm rise	214	214	214

Mean salinity for October is shown along the river moving upstream from the mouth to the head of the estuary for 2002 (dry year; fig. 14A) and 2005 (typical year; fig. 14B). Figure 14 was created by running the model, and for each river km, recording the mean salinity for the 31 days of October at that point along the river. This process was followed for the no-rise scenario and each of the three sea-level rise scenarios.

Salinity is similar at the mouth of the river for both years (fig. 14). Farther upstream, however, salinity is higher for a dry year (2002; fig. 14A) than for a typical year (2005; fig. 14B), again demonstrating the role of river flow in pushing the salinity back toward the bay. For the 50-cm sea-level rise scenario, salinity is 15 ppt at river km 39 for 2005, and the model predicted the same salinity at river km 45 for 2002, indicating a 6-km upstream migration.

The increase in salinity for each sea-level rise scenario is somewhat uniform spatially, with the largest change at the head of the estuary. For both years, at the head of the York estuary (river km 52), a large increase in mean salinity is predicted for each sea-level rise scenario (fig. 14). This will greatly alter the existing water-quality gradients between the brackish water and freshwater.

Chickahominy River

Results for the Chickahominy River simulations are presented for just downstream of Walkers Dam (fig. 4), the approximate location of the municipal drinking-water intake for the City of Newport News. During a wet year at this location, salinity is not expected to exceed 0.1 ppt for any of the sea-level rise scenarios (table 4). During a typical year, salinity may exceed 0.1 ppt for fewer than 100 days (table 4). In contrast, during a dry year when river flow is lower, salinity may

Despite month, year, or amount of sea-level rise, the most saline water in all cases is in the deepest part of the channel and the least saline water is on the surface of the southwest side of the river (figs. 11, 12, 13). The southwest side of the river is dominated by discharge from the Pamunkey River, which has a larger drainage basin (3,812 square kilometers, km²) than that of the Mattaponi River (2,362 km²). Nevertheless, with sea-level rise, salinity increases even in the southwest side of the river. Salinity is greatly reduced during a wet year (2003), even at depth. The primary difference among the three figures is that September and October show the most saline conditions, followed by July and August, with the least salinity in November and December.

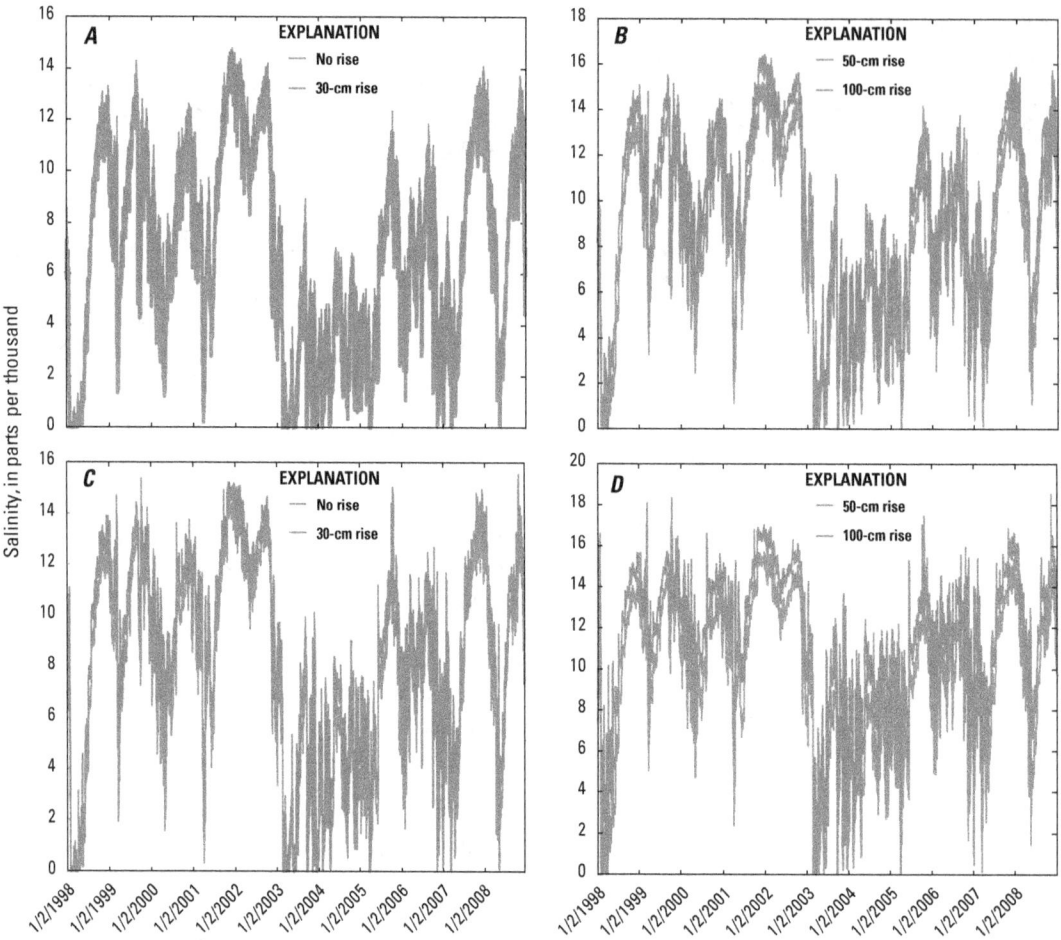

Figure 10.   Time series of surface and bottom simulated salinity at the head of the York estuary for three sea-level rise scenarios, 1998–2008; *A*, no rise and 30-cm rise at surface; *B*, 50-cm rise and 100-cm rise at surface; *C*, no rise and 30-cm rise at bottom; and *D*, 50-cm rise and 100-cm rise at bottom.

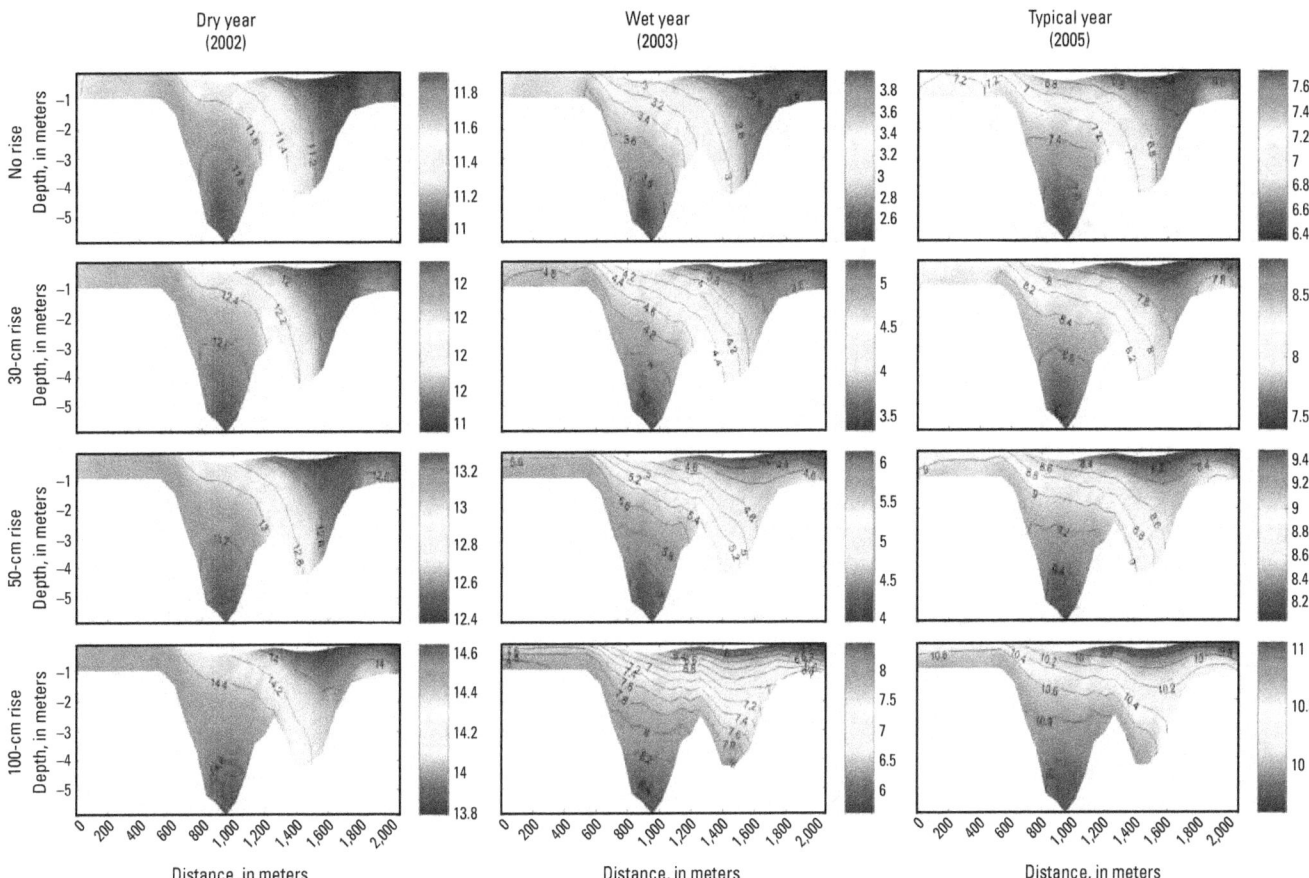

Figure 11. Cross sections (*A–A'* on figure 4) of average simulated salinity at the head of the York estuary for July and August. Salinity units (right axis) in parts per thousand.

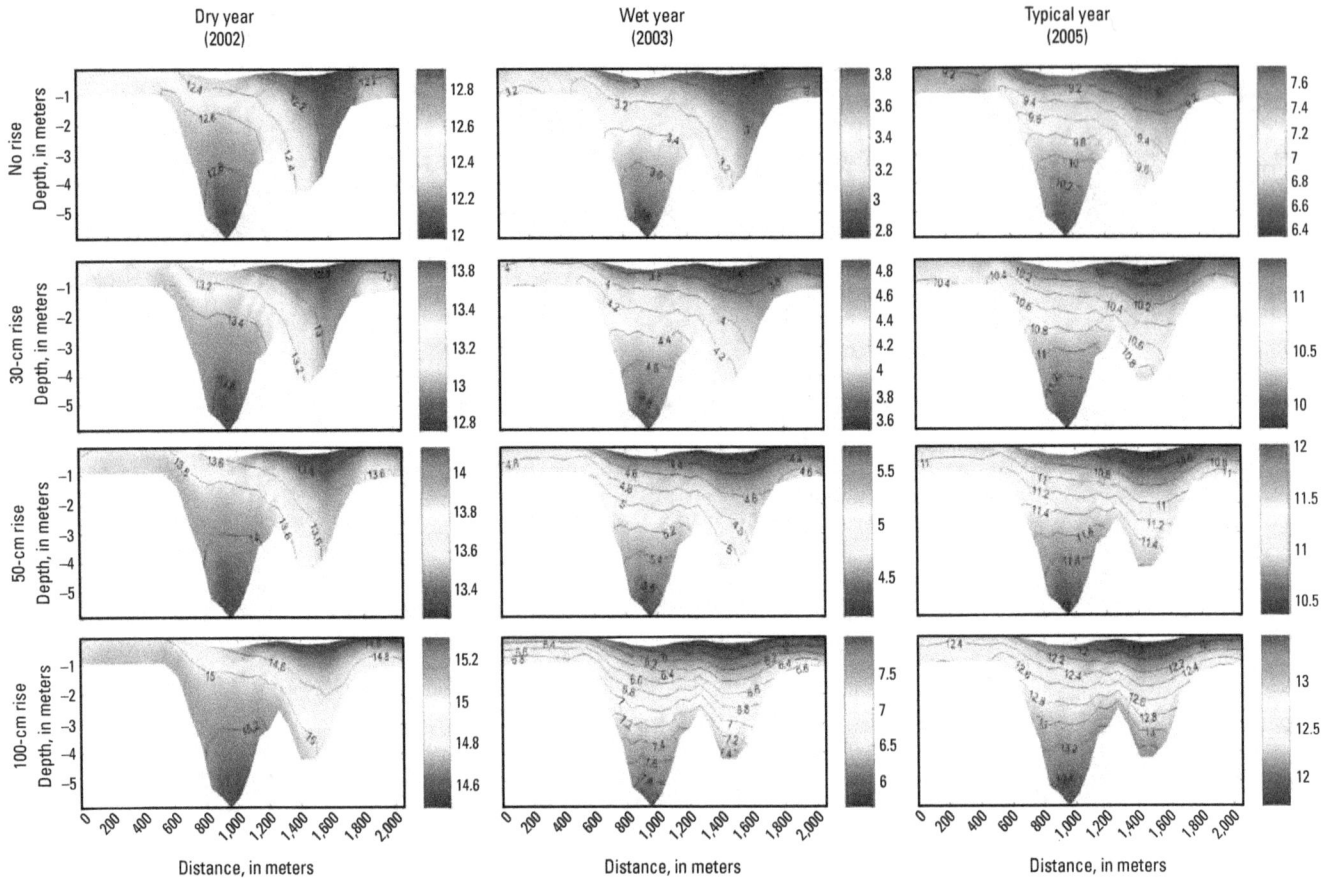

Figure 12.   Cross sections (*A–A'* on figure 4) of average simulated salinity at the head of the York estuary for September and October. Salinity units (right axis) in parts per thousand.

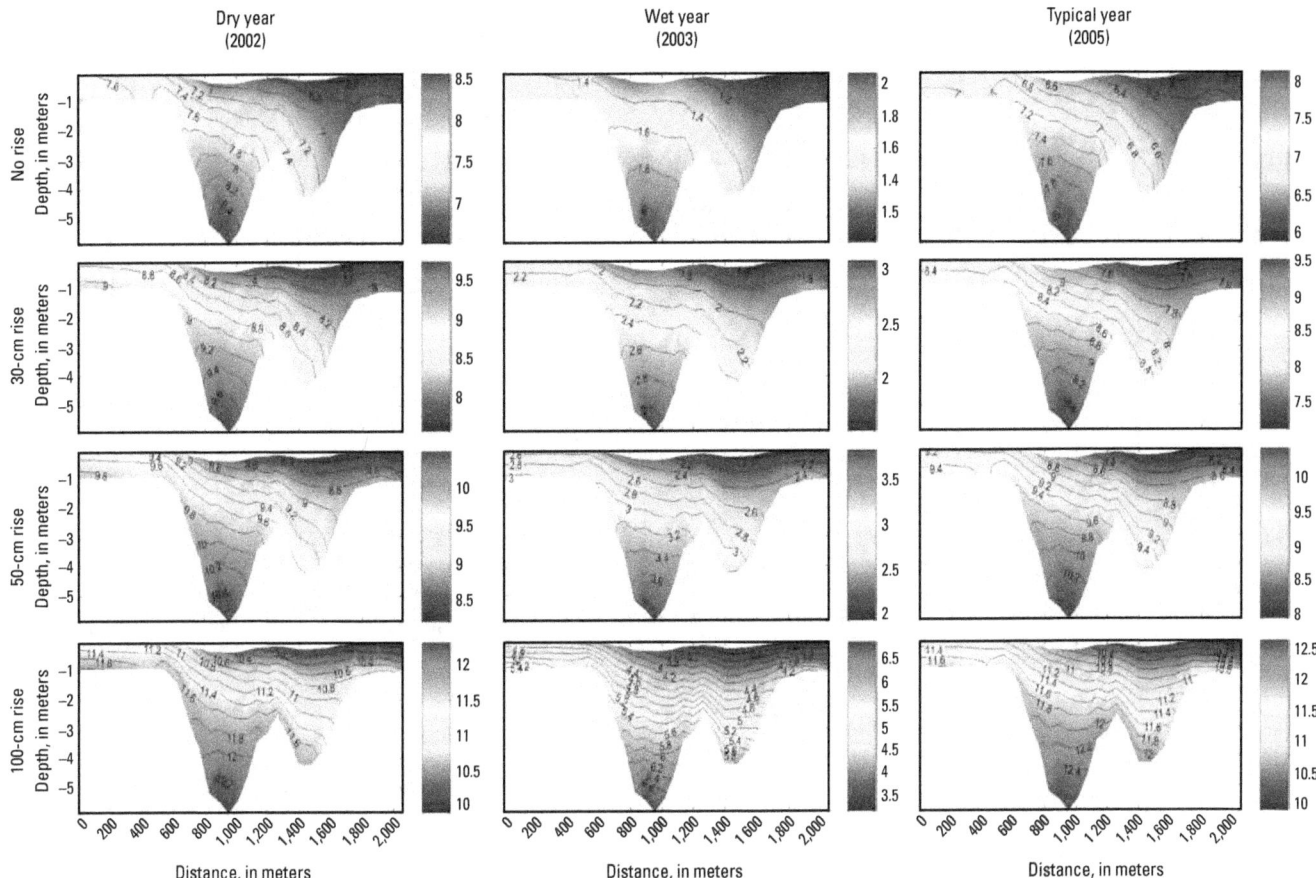

Figure 13. Cross sections (*A–A'* on figure 4) of average simulated salinity at the head of the York estuary for November and December. Salinity units (right axis) in parts per thousand.

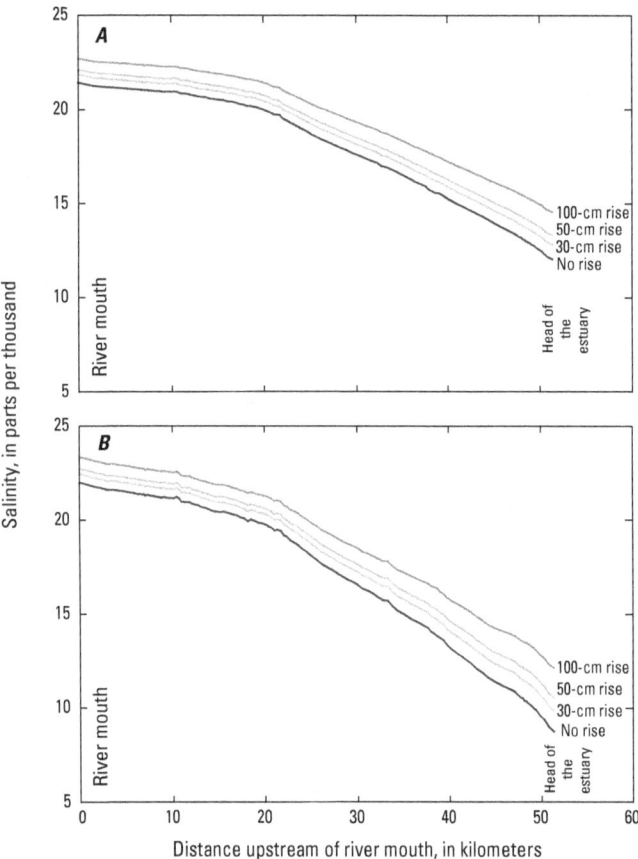

Figure 14.   Effect of simulated sea-level rise scenarios on 31-day mean salinity along the York River; *A*, October 2002, dry-year scenario; *B*, October 2005, typical-year scenario.

Table 4.   Number of days that salinity is predicted to exceed 0.1 parts per thousand at Walkers Dam on the Chickahominy River from June 1 to December 31 (total 214 days) of the year indicated for the no-rise scenario and the three sea-level rise scenarios.

[cm, centimeter]

Model scenario	Dry year 2002	Wet year 2003	Typical year 2005
No rise	69	0	2
30-cm rise	106	0	11
50-cm rise	131	0	20
100-cm rise	194	0	71

Table 5.   Number of days that water from sea-level rise is predicted to overtop Walkers Dam on the Chickahominy River from June 1 to December 31 (total 214 days) of the year indicated for the no-rise scenario and the three sea-level rise scenarios.

[cm, centimeter]

Model scenario	Dry year 2002	Wet year 2003	Typical year 2005
No rise	1	22	17
30-cm rise	44	133	120
50-cm rise	138	190	195
100-cm rise	214	214	214

exceed 0.1 ppt for all three of the sea-level rise scenarios, with the number of days increasing with increasing sea-level rise (table 4). In addition to elevated salinity at the dam, overtopping of the dam by increasing tide levels is a drinking water-supply concern (table 5).

The time-series salinity data for the no-rise scenario and the three sea-level rise scenarios suggest that salinity increases most dramatically with the highest sea-level rise scenario (fig. 15) and less so with lower rises at both the surface and the bottom of the river. For example, on October 2, 2005 (typical year), salinity at the surface for no rise is 0.005 ppt, and is 0.005, 0.014, and 2.46 ppt for a 30-, 50-, and 100-cm rise, respectively. Salinity is highest during a dry year (2002) and decreases substantially during a wet year (2003; fig. 15). For example, on October 2, 2002 (dry year), salinity at the surface for no rise is 0.695 ppt, and is 2.07, 2.96, and 5.50 ppt for a 30-, 50-, and 100-cm rise, respectively. This simulation is in contrast to October 2, 2003 (wet year), when salinity at the surface is 0.014 ppt for all sea-level rise scenarios and for the no-rise scenario. For a 100-cm rise during a dry year, surface salinity greater than 1 ppt would endure for an 8-month period. These data suggest that sea-level rise will significantly affect the drinking-water supply intake.

Salinity distributions for cross section *B–B'*, just downstream of Walkers Dam, are shown for average salinity for July and August (fig. 16); September and October (fig. 17); and November and December (fig. 18); the scale for salinity is not uniform for all panels in these figures. The cross section (*B–B'*) is viewed looking upstream (the left side of the section is the northwest side of the river).

Despite month, year, or amount of sea-level rise, the most saline water in all cases is in the deepest part of the channel and the least saline water is on the surface of the river (figs. 16, 17, 18). Salinity is greatly reduced during a wet year (2003), even at depth. In a dry year with a 100-cm sea-level rise, however, average September and October salinity would increase nearly tenfold from 0.5 ppt with no rise to 5 ppt with a 100-cm rise. The primary difference among the three figures is that September and October show the most saline conditions, followed by July and August, with the least salinity in November and December.

Model simulations show that river discharge acts as a barrier to upstream salinity migration (fig. 19). Mean salinity for October is shown along the river moving upstream from the mouth of Chickahominy River for 2002 (dry year; fig. 19*A*) and 2005 (typical year; fig. 19*B*). Salinity is 4 ppt higher at the mouth of the river for the dry year (2002) than for the typical

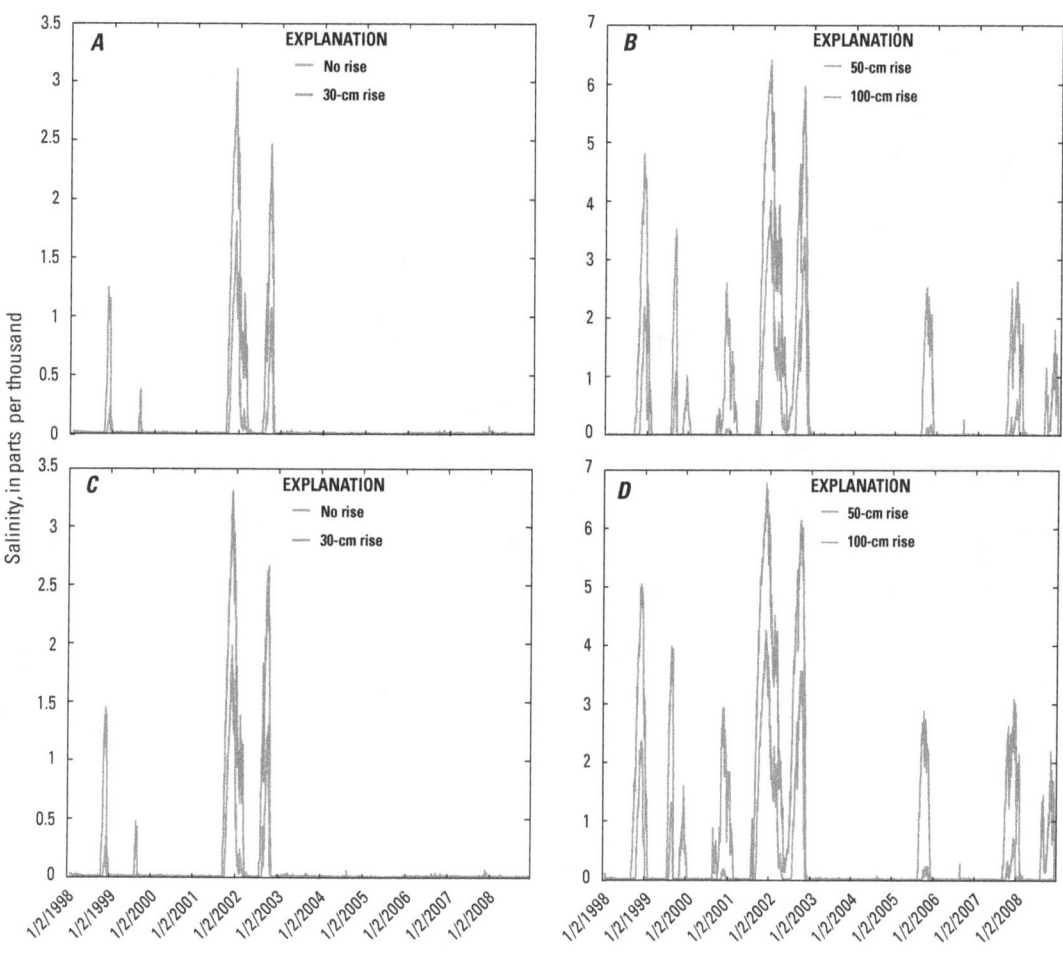

Figure 15.   Time series of simulated surface and bottom salinity at Walkers Dam on the Chickahominy River for three sea-level rise scenarios, 1998–2008; *A*, no rise and 30-cm rise at surface; *B*, 50-cm rise and 100-cm rise at surface; *C*, no rise and 30-cm rise at bottom; *D*, 50-cm rise and 100-cm rise at bottom.

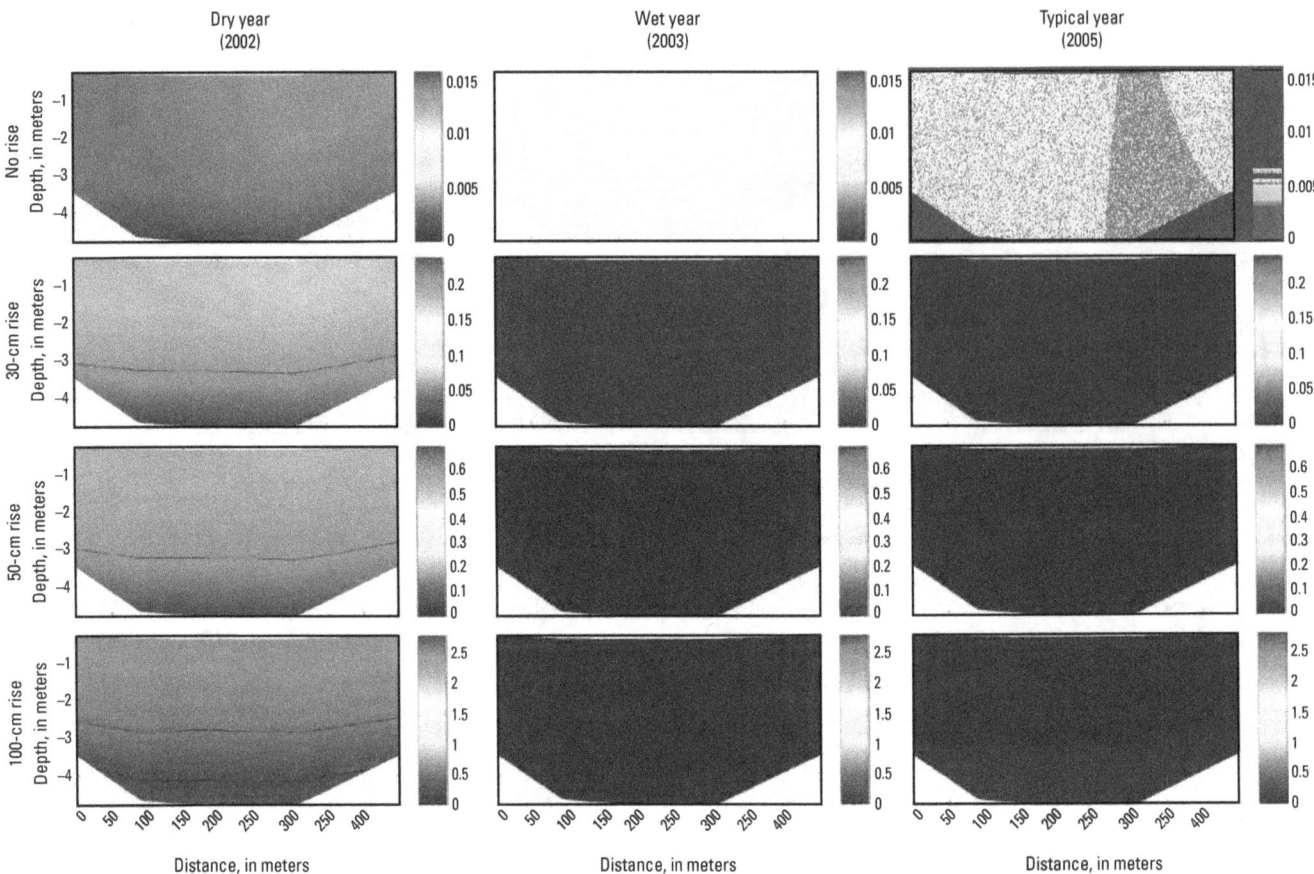

Figure 16.   Cross sections (*B–B'* on fig. 4) of average simulated salinity downstream of Walkers Dam on the Chickahominy River for July and August. Salinity units (right axis) in parts per thousand.

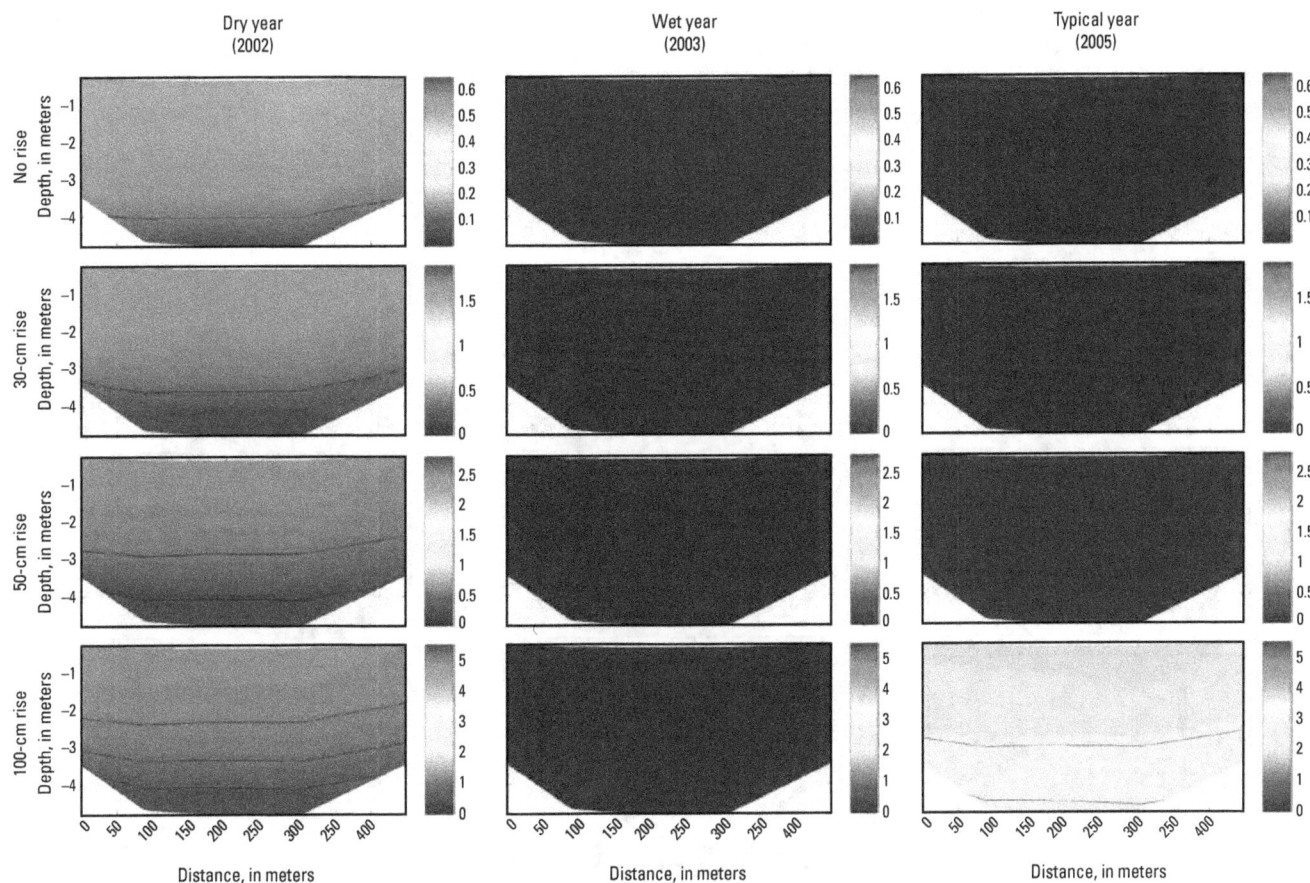

Figure 17. Cross sections (*B–B'* on fig. 4) of average simulated salinity downstream of Walkers Dam on the Chickahominy River for September and October. Salinity units (right axis) in parts per thousand.

year (2005) for the no-rise scenario and for the three sea-level rise scenarios. For the 50-cm sea-level rise scenario, salinity is 4 ppt at river km 13 for 2005; the model predicted the same salinity at river km 28 for 2002, indicating a 15-km upstream migration for a dry year relative to a typical year. Near Walkers Dam, for a dry year (2002) salinity is predicted to more

than double for all three sea-level rise scenarios, relative to a typical year (fig. 19). During a typical year near Walkers Dam, salinity is predicted to increase to 0.006 ppt, 0.07 ppt, and more than 2 ppt for the 30-, 50-, and 100-cm rise scenarios, respectively (fig. 19B).

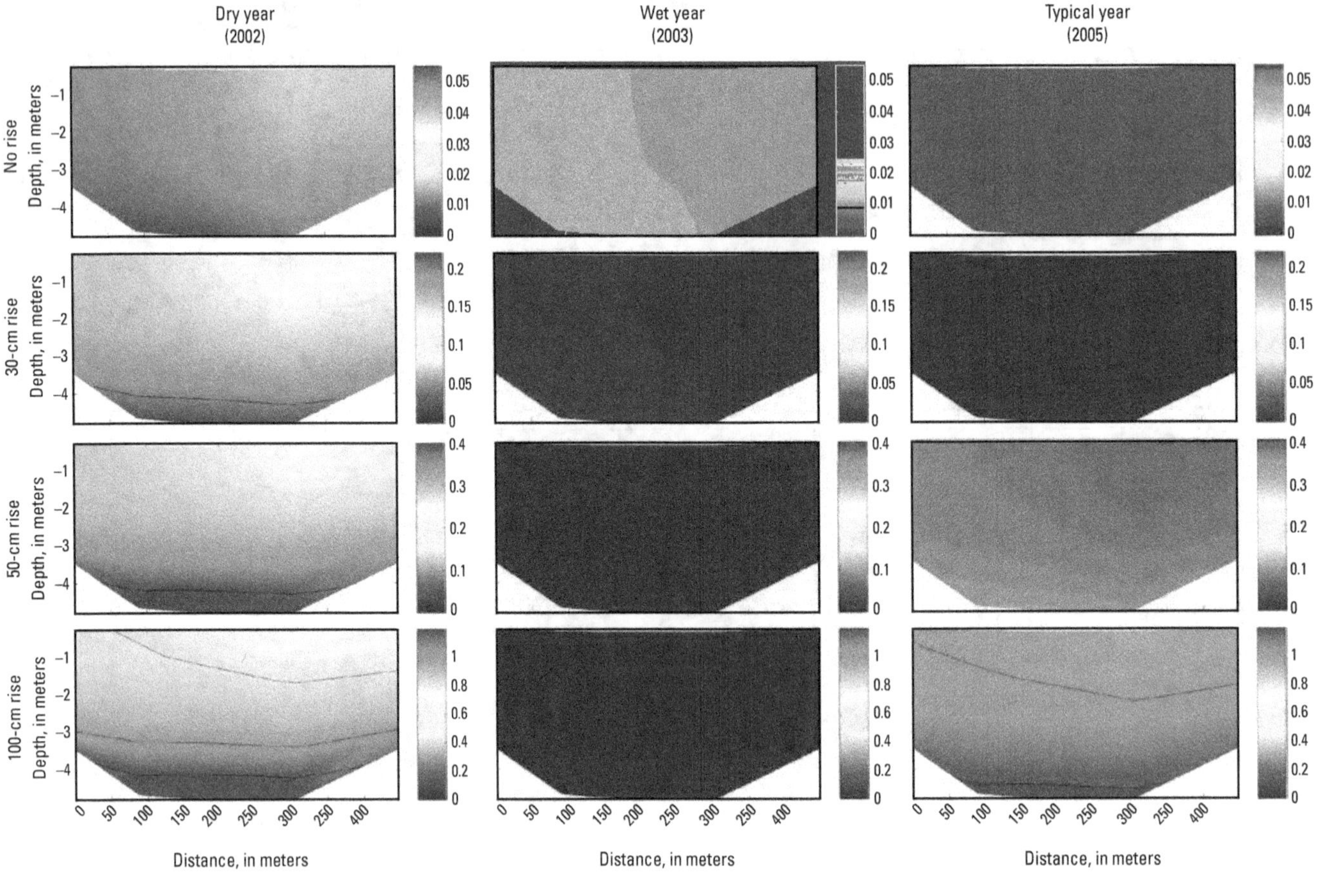

Figure 18.   Cross sections (*B–B′* on fig. 4) of average simulated salinity downstream of Walkers Dam on the Chickahominy River for November and December. Salinity units (right axis) in parts per thousand.

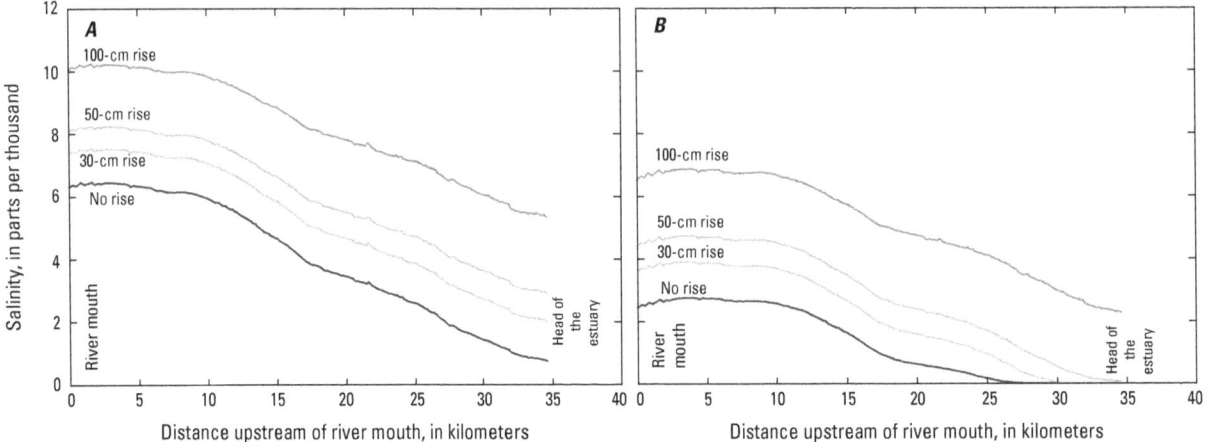

Figure 19.   Effect of simulated sea-level rise scenarios on 31-day mean salinity along the Chickahominy River; *A*, October 2002, dry-year scenario; *B*, October 2005, typical-year scenario.

Summary

Earth has a long history of a changing climate and, as a result, changing sea levels. Currently, sea level is rising along the Atlantic coast of the eastern United States at a rate higher than the global rate. Sea-level rise can affect coastal and estuarine areas in several ways, including causing increased damage from storms and flooding, changes in the existence and distribution of wetlands, and encroachment of saline water into estuaries and coastal aquifers. Of particular importance to drinking-water utilities is saline water that has migrated far enough upstream to affect drinking-water supplies.

One of the first steps in becoming a climate-ready utility is to define and understand how future changes in climate could affect local and regional water resources. The U.S. Geological Survey, in cooperation with the City of Newport News, Virginia, undertook a study to evaluate the effects of potential future sea-level rise on two Virginia estuaries. The study focused on the York River and Chickahominy/James River estuaries, which delineate Virginia's Lower Peninsula. For the magnitude of potential sea-level rise for the mid-Atlantic region, the study relied on the U.S. Climate Change Science Program, which synthesized an enormous amount of climatic and oceanic modeling to propose three future sea-level rise scenarios for the 21st century. The scenarios were developed from a combination of the 20th century relative sea-level rise rate and either a 2 or 7 millimeter per year (mm/yr) increase in global sea level:

- Scenario 1: The 20th century rate, which is generally 3 to 4 mm/yr in the mid-Atlantic region (30 to 40 centimeters (cm) total by the year 2100);

- Scenario 2: The 20th century rate plus 2 mm/yr acceleration (up to 50 cm total by 2100); and

- Scenario 3: The 20th century rate plus 7 mm/yr acceleration (up to 100 cm total by 2100).

This report refers to the three scenarios as the 30-cm, the 50-cm, and the 100-cm rise, respectively. The scenarios do not consider any future changes in freshwater flows in the York and Chickahominy/James Rivers.

Simulations were made by use of the Three-Dimensional Hydrodynamic-Eutrophication Model (HEM-3D), developed by the Virginia Institute of Marine Science. HEM-3D was used to simulate tides, tidal currents, and salinity for the Chesapeake Bay to produce boundaries for simulating these parameters for the York River and the Chickahominy/James River. To address salinity change from potential sea-level rise, a nested-grid modeling approach was used to accurately simulate salinity with sufficient resolution while not sacrificing computational efficiency. A sensitivity analysis of the model indicated that the model was most sensitive to a decrease in river discharge and change of salinity concentration at the open boundary. The model also is sensitive to wind and change of bottom roughness.

Model results for both estuaries indicated that high freshwater river flow was effective in pushing the salinity back toward Chesapeake Bay. The results also indicated that large increases in mean salinity are predicted for each sea-level rise scenario. Model results for both estuaries indicated that the months of September and October have the most saline conditions, followed by July and August, with the least salinity in November and December. These results are consistent whether the year is wet, dry, or typical, and whether sea level does not rise, or rises 30, 50, or 100 cm.

For the 50-cm sea-level rise scenario on the York River during a typical year, the model simulation showed a salinity of 15 ppt at river km 39. During a dry year, the same salinity (15 ppt) was simulated at river km 45, which means that saltwater was shown to migrate 6 km farther upstream. The same was true of the Chickahominy River for the 50-cm sea-level rise scenario but to a greater degree; a salinity of 4 ppt was simulated at river km 13 during a typical year and at river km 28 during a dry year, indicating that saltwater migrated 15 km farther upstream during a dry year.

Increases in mean salinity will greatly alter the existing water-quality gradients between the brackish water and freshwater. This is particularly important for the Chickahominy River, where a drinking-water-supply intake for the City of Newport News is located. The methodologies developed as part of this study are transferable to other tributary basins to the bay. The results of this study can be expanded and refined to assess the effect of sea-level rise throughout the Chesapeake Bay estuary.

Acknowledgments

The authors express their appreciation to Ron Harris, Chief of Water Resources of the Newport News Waterworks, who supported and guided this project to its successful completion. We thank Bo Hong, Virginia Institute of Marine Science, for conducting much of the estuarine modeling and processing the model results. We also appreciate the colleague reviews provided by Eric Swain and Paul Conrads, U.S. Geological Survey, of an earlier draft of the report.

References

Ayers, M.A., Wolock, D.M., McCabe, G.J., Hay, L.E., and Tasker, G.D., 1994, Sensitivity of water resources in the Delaware River Basin to climate variability and change: U.S. Geological Survey Water-Supply Paper 2422, 42 p.

Bates, B.C., Kundzewicz, Z.W., Wu, S., and Palutikof, J.P., eds., 2008, Climate change and water: Technical Paper of the Intergovernmental Panel on Climate Change, IPCC Secretariat, Geneva, Switzerland.

Blumberg, A.F., and Mellor, G.M., 1987, A description of a three-dimensional coastal ocean circulation model, *in* Heaps, N.S., ed., Three-dimensional coastal ocean models, Coastal and Estuarine Science: Washington, D.C., American Geophysical Union, v. 4, p. 1–19.

Boon, J., Wang, H., and Shen, J., 2008, Planning for sea level rise and coastal flooding: Available at *http://www.vims.edu/research/centers/programs/icccr/_docs/index.php*.

Brekke, L.D., Kiang, J.E., Olsen, J.R., Pulwarty, R.S., Raff, D.A., Turnipseed, D.P., Webb, R.S., and White, K.D., 2009, Climate change and water resources management—A federal perspective: U.S. Geological Survey Circular 1331, 65 p. Available at *http://pubs.usgs.gov/circ/1331/*.

Chand, D., Wood, R., Anderson, T.L., Satheesh, S.K., Charlson, R.J., 2009, Satellite-derived direct radiative effects of aerosols dependent on cloud cover: Nature Geoscience, v. 2, p. 181–184, DOI: 10.1038/NGEO437.

Climate Change Science Program, 2009, Coastal sensitivity to sea-level rise—A focus on the mid-Atlantic region, *in* Titus, J.G. (coordinating lead author), Anderson, K.E., Cahoon, D.R., Gesch, D.B., Gill, S.K., Gutierrez, B.T., Theiler, E.R., and Williams, S.J. (lead authors), Report by the U.S. Climate Change Science Program and the Subcommittee on Global Change Research: Washington, D.C., U.S. Environmental Protection Agency, 320 p. Available at *http://www.epa.gov/climatechange/effects/coastal/sap4-1.html*.

Esper, J., Cook, E.R., and Schweingruber, F.H., 2002, Low-frequency signals in long tree-ring chronologies for reconstructing past temperature variability: Science, v. 295, p. 2250–2253.

Galperin, B., Kantha, L.H., Hassis, S., and Rosati, A., 1988, A quasi-equilibrium turbulent energy model for geophysical flows: Journal of the Atmospheric Sciences, v. 45, p. 55–62.

Gibson, J.R., and Najjar, R.G., 2000, The response of Chesapeake Bay salinity to climate-induced changes in streamflow: Limnology and Oceanography, v. 45, p. 1764–1772.

Hamrick, J.M., 1992, A three-dimensional environmental fluid dynamics computer code—Theoretical and computational aspects: Special report in applied marine science and ocean engineering: College of William and Mary, VIMS, no. 317, 63 p.

Hegerl, G.C., Crowley, T.J., Hyde, W.T., and Frame, D.J. 2006, Climate sensitivity constrained by temperature reconstructions over the past seven centuries: Nature, v. 440, p. 1029–1032.

Hilton, T.W., Najjar, R.G., Zhong, L., and Li, M., 2008, Is there a signal of sea-level rise in Chesapeake Bay salinity?: Journal of Geophysical Research, v. 113, C09002.

Huang, S.P., Pollack, H.N., and Shen, P.-Y., 2000, Temperature trends over the past five centuries reconstructed from borehole temperatures: Nature, v. 403, no. 6771, p. 756–758.

Hull, C.H.J., and Titus, J.G., eds., 1986, Greenhouse effect, sea level rise, and salinity in the Delaware estuary: U.S. Environmental Protection Agency, EPA-230-05-86-010 (1999 Internet Version), 36 p.

Huybrechts, Phillippe, 2002, Sea-level changes at the LGM from ice-dynamic reconstructions of the Greenland and Antarctic ice sheets during the glacial cycles, 203-231 (Copyright [2002], with permission from Elsevier.)

Intergovernmental Panel on Climate Change, 2007, Climate change 2007—The physical science basis, *in* Solomon, S., Qin, D., Manning, M., Chen, Z., Marquis, M., Averyt, K.B., Tignor, M., and Miller, H.L., eds., Contribution of Working Group I to the Fourth Assessment Report of the Intergovernmental Panel on Climate Change: Cambridge, United Kingdom, Cambridge University Press. Available at *http://www.ipcc.ch/ipccreports/ar4-wg1.htm*.

Jones, P.D., Osborn, T.J., Briffa, K.R., Folland, C.K., Horton, E.B., Alexander, L.V., Parker, D.E., and Rayner, N.A., 2001, Adjusting for sampling density in grid box land and ocean surface temperature time series: Journal of Geophysical Research, v. 106, p. 3371–3380.

MacFarlane, B.J., and Walberg, E.J., 2010, Climate change in Hampton Roads—Impacts and stakeholder involvement: Hampton Roads Planning District Commission, 43 p.

Mann, M.E., and Jones, P.D., 2003, 2,000 Year hemispheric multi-proxy temperature reconstructions: IGBP PAGES/World Data Center for Paleoclimatology Data Contribution Series #2003-051: Boulder, Colo., NOAA/NGDC Paleoclimatology Program.

Mellor, G.L., and Yamada, T., 1982, Development of a turbulence closure model for geophysical fluid problems: Reviews of Geophysics and Space Physics, v. 20, p. 851–875.

Miller, Kathleen, and Yates, David, 2006, Climate change and water resources—A primer for municipal water providers: AWWA Research Foundation.

Moberg, A., Sonechkin, D.M., Holmgren, K., Datsenko, N.M., and Karlen, W., 2005, 2,000-Year Northern Hemisphere temperature reconstruction: IGBP PAGES/World Data Center for Paleoclimatology Data. Contribution Series #2005-019. Boulder, Colo., NOAA/NGDC Paleoclimatology Program.

Muhs, D.R., Wehmiller, J.F., Simmons, K.R., and York, L.L., 2004, Quaternary sea-level history of the United States: Quaternary period in the United States, v. 1, p. 147–183.

Najjar, R.G., Pyke, C.R., Adams, M.B., Breitburg, D., Hershner, C., Kemp, M., Howarth, R., Mulholland, M.R., Paolisso, M., Secor, D., Sellner, K., Wardrop, D., Wood, R., 2010, Potential climate-change impacts on the Chesapeake Bay: Estuarine, Coastal and Shelf Science, v. 86, p. 1–20.

National Oceanic and Atmospheric Administration, 2010, Sea-level trends, Tides and currents: Accessed June 8, 2010, at *http://tidesandcurrents.noaa.gov/sltrends/sltrends_station.shtml?stnid=8638610.*

National Research Council, 1987, Responding to changes in sea level—Engineering implications: Committee on Engineering Implications of Changes in Relative Mean Sea Level, Marine Board, National Research Council, 160 p. Available at *http://www.nap.edu/catalog.php?record_id=1006.*

National Research Council, 2006, Surface temperature reconstruction for the last 2,000 years: Washington, D.C., National Academies Press, 160 p. Available at *http://www.nap.edu/catalog.php?record_id=11676.*

Oerlemans, J., 2005, Global glacier length temperature reconstruction: IGBP PAGES/World Data Center for Paleoclimatology, Data Contribution Series #2005-059: Boulder, Colo., NOAA/NCDC Paleoclimatology Program.

Overpeck, J.T., Otto-Bliesner, B.L., Miller, G.H., Muhs, D.R., Alley, R.B., and Kiehl, J.T., 2006, Paleoclimatic evidence for future ice-sheet instability and rapid sea-level rise: Science, v. 311, no. 5768, p. 1747–1750. DOI: 10.1126/science.1115159.

Park, K., Kuo, A.Y., Shen, J., and Hamrick, J.M., 1995, A three-dimensional hydrodynamic eutrophication model (HEM-3D)—Description of water quality and sediment process submodels: Special report in Applied Marine Science and Ocean Engineering: Gloucester Point, Va., Virginia Institute of Marine Science, no. 327, p. 102.

Petit, J.R., Raynaud, D., Lorius, C., Jouzel, J., Delaygue, G., Barkov, N.I., and Kotlyakov, V.M., 2000, Historical isotopic temperature record from the Vostok ice core, *in* Trends—A compendium of data on global change: Oak Ridge, Tenn., Carbon Dioxide Information Analysis Center, Oak Ridge National Laboratory, U.S. Department of Energy, DOI: 10.3334/CDIAC/cli.006.

Poff, N.L., Brinson, M.M., and Day, J.W., Jr., 2002, Aquatic ecosystems and global climate change: Pew Center on Global Climate Change, 45 p. Available at *http://rydberg.biology.colostate.edu/~poff/Public/poffpubs/Poff2002(PEW_AquaticEcosys).pdf.*

Pope, J.P., and Burbey, T.J., 2004, Multiple-aquifer characterization from single borehole extensometer records: Ground Water, v. 42, p. 45–58.

Schubel, J.R., and Pritchard, D.W., 1986, Responses of upper Chesapeake Bay to variations in discharge of the Susquehanna River: Estuaries, v. 9, no. 4A, p. 236–249.

Shen, J., Boon, J.D., and Kuo, A.Y., 1999, A modeling study of a tidal intrusion front and its impact on larval dispersion in the James River estuary, Virginia: Estuaries, v. 22, no. 3A, p. 681–692.

Shen, J., and Haas, L., 2004, Calculating age and residence time in the tidal York River using three-dimensional model experiments: Estuarine, Coastal and Shelf Science, v. 61, no. 3, p. 449–461.

Shen, J., and Lin, J., 2006, Modeling study of the influences of tide and stratification on age of water in the tidal James River: Estuarine, Coastal and Shelf Science, v. 68, no. 1–2, p. 101–112.

Sisson, G.M., Shen, J., Kim, S.C., Kuo, A.Y., and Boon, J.D., 1997, VIMS three-dimensional hydrodynamic-eutrophication model (HEM-3D)—Application of the hydrodynamic model to the York River system: Gloucester Point, Va., Virginia Institute of Marine Science, Special report in Applied Marine Science and Ocean Engineering, no. 341.

Williams, S.J., Gutierrez, B.T., Titus, J.G., Gill, S.K., Cahoon, D.R., Thieler, E.R., Anderson, K.E., FitzGerald, D., Burkett, V., and Samenow, J., 2009, Sea-level rise and its effects on the coast, *in* Titus, J.G. (coordinating lead author), Anderson, K.E., Cahoon, D.R., Gesch, D.B., Gill, S.K., Gutierrez, B.T., Thieler, E.R., and Williams, S.J. (lead authors), Coastal sensitivity to sea-level rise—A focus on the mid-Atlantic region: Washington, D.C., U.S. Climate Change Science Program and the Subcommittee on Global Change Research, U.S. Environmental Protection Agency, p. 11–24.

Appendix

The appendix includes sections on Model Performance, Salinity Verification for the Chickahominy River model, and Model Sensitivity for the Chickahominy/James River model.

Model Performance

Model performance was evaluated using over 10 years of salinity observation data collected by the Chesapeake Bay Program. Monthly salinity data collected at different depths were downloaded from the Chesapeake Bay Program website (*http://www.chesapeakebay.net*). Modeled surface and bottom salinity at selected locations along the main channel of each estuary were examined. The salinity variation inside the estuary is highly dependent upon the river discharge into the lower Chesapeake Bay. A strong seasonal variation was observed,

with elevated salinity in summer and lower salinity in spring. The evaluation of the model was focused on the model performance and its ability to simulate spring-neap and seasonal salinity variations, particularly during dry and wet years. The model simulations for seasonal and long-term salinity changes were consistent with actual observations. The stratification/destratification processes shown by the observed data are reflected in the modeled time series results and indicated that model simulations of the estuarine circulation are consistent.

Salinity Verification for Chickahominy River

Simulated salinity data along the Chickahominy River were compared to data from four existing salinity observation stations operated by Newport News Waterworks (fig. 1-1). The observation data were collected about 0.3 m below the water

Figure 1-1. Locations of salinity observation stations in the Chickahominy River.

surface. Model results for the surface and bottom and observations for salinity are shown for salinity monitoring stations at the Rt. 5 Bridge (fig. 1-2), Chickahominy Haven (fig. 1-3), Riverside Camp (fig. 1-4), and Walkers Dam (fig. 1-5). The model estimated the salinity at both the Rt. 5 Bridge and Chickahominy Haven stations reasonably well but slightly over estimated the salinity in a few cases farther upstream, at Riverside Camp and Walkers Dam.

Model Sensitivity

Hydrodynamic model performance is dependent upon, among other things, the model calibration to parameters that numerically approximate the underlying physical processes and the forcing conditions used for driving the model at the open boundary. Both the eddy viscosity and diffusivity are key parameters for a hydrodynamic model. The hydrodynamic part

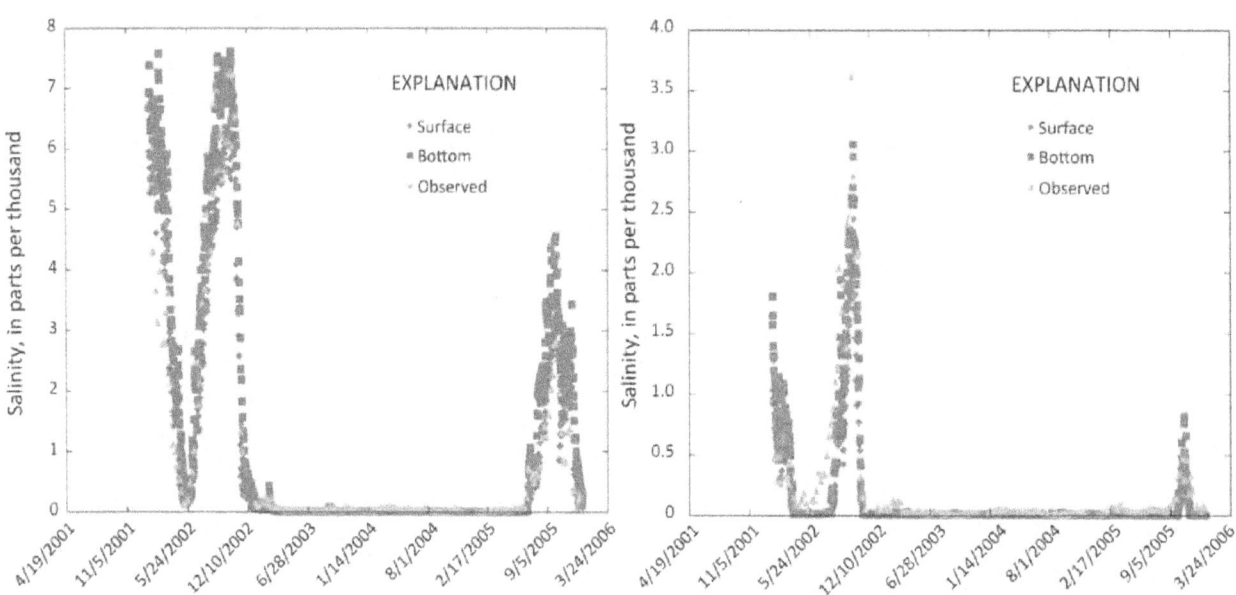

Figure 1-2.   Comparison of simulated and observed salinity at Rt. 5 Bridge station.

Figure 1-4.   Comparison of simulated and observed salinity at Riverside Camp station.

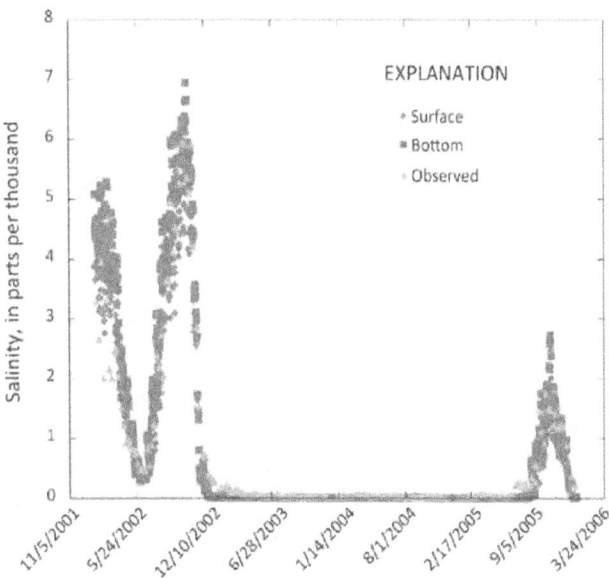

Figure 1-3.   Comparison of simulated and observed salinity at Chickahominy Haven station.

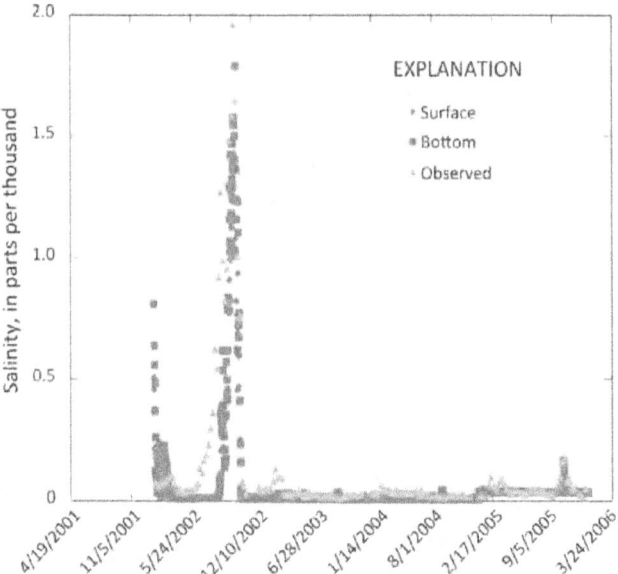

Figure 1-5.   Comparison of simulated and observed salinity at Walkers Dam station.

of the model uses the Mellor and Yamada level 2.5 turbulence closure scheme (Mellor and Yamada, 1982; Galperin and others, 1988) and computes both eddy viscosity and diffusivity based on transport of turbulent length and intensity. For bottom roughness, the model uses the logarithmic profile to compute the bottom shear stress based on prescribed bottom roughness values. Constant bottom roughness values of 0.2 centimeter (cm) for the York River and 0.15 cm for the James River were used in the models based on the calibrations to surface elevations. The model used U.S. Geological Survey discharge data at the river boundary and National Oceanic and Atmospheric Administration wind data at the surface boundary. For the open-boundary condition at the mouth of each river, the model used tide and salinity data resulting from simulations by a large-domain Chesapeake Bay model. Any deviation of the forcing data from the real conditions can result in discrepancies between model simulations and observations.

To assess the model performance and model sensitivity with respect to model parameter and forcing conditions, four sensitivity tests were performed for the model simulation of the Chickahominy/James River for the year 2001. A model base case was formulated for the simulation run without changing parameters or boundary conditions, which is equivalent to model calibration. The four sensitivity tests were:

- Test 1: Decrease river discharge by 20 percent;

- Test 2: Decrease salinity concentration at the open boundary by 15 percent;

- Test 3: Increase bottom roughness by 100 percent;

- Test 4: Decrease wind forcing on the surface by 100 percent.

Model sensitivity was evaluated with the Chickahominy/James River model. Results of these sensitivity tests, however, should be representative for the model performance in all Chesapeake Bay tributaries. The model simulation started at day 300 in year 2000 with the forcings that were used for the model calibration and was run for 60 days. The forcings were changed starting January 1, 2001, and the model was run for one year. To test the sensitivity of bottom roughness, the value was changed and the model was run starting from day 300 of year 2000 and allowed to proceed 370 days. The results of the sensitivity tests were compared to those of the base case.

Sensitivity to River Discharge (Test 1)

To evaluate the model sensitivity to river discharge, time series of salinities at the "Chickahominy," "LE5.1," and "RET5.2" stations were compared (fig. 1-6A, B, C; see fig. 9 in body of report for locations of the salinity stations). As expected, decreasing river discharge by 20 percent allowed the salinity to migrate farther into the estuary. The salinity at the Chickahominy station increased about 1.0–1.5 parts per thousand (ppt) at both the surface and bottom (fig. 1-7). Salinity

is more sensitive to the decrease of river discharge along the main channel of the James River, where the maximum salinity change was about 5 ppt. The 2 ppt salinity contour moved upstream about 5 kilometers (km) relative to the base case (fig. 1-8 Base Case, and Test 1). The results of Test 1 suggest that the salinity distribution is very sensitive to river discharge.

Sensitivity to Salinity Open-Boundary Condition (Test 2)

The accuracy of salinity simulations is highly dependent upon the salinity specification at the model open-boundary condition. The hourly model salinity boundary conditions were obtained from a large Chesapeake Bay model. The Chesapeake Bay model open boundary is located far away from the bay mouth and was specified using climatology salinity conditions, which are the long-term monthly mean salinity concentrations obtained from a global model output. The Chesapeake Bay model salinity calibration shows that the model is not very sensitive to the salinity specification at the open boundary. This may not be true, however, when simulating tributaries using the nested-grid modeling approach. To test this, a sensitivity analysis was conducted with the salinity concentration at the model open boundary condition reduced by 15 percent. The model is very sensitive to the salinity open boundary specification (fig. 1-6). With a 15-percent decrease in salinity concentration at the open boundary condition, the salinity decreased substantially along the James River. The maximum salinity difference was up to 4 ppt in the Chickahominy River, and it was more than 6 ppt within the channel of the James River (fig. 1-7). The salinity change along the James River is much greater than the 15 percent that was used for the change of salinity near the mouth. The mean salinity contour of 2 ppt moved downstream by approximately 10 km (figure 1-8A, and C).

Sensitivity to Bottom Roughness (Test 3)

Bottom roughness is the only estimated parameter used during model calibration to surface elevation. A constant roughness of 0.2 cm was used in the James River model. The model sensitivity to a change in bottom roughness was conducted by doubling the value. The model is very sensitive to the bottom roughness and its effects on tidal propagation along the estuary (fig. 1-9 Base Case, and Test 1). With an increase of the bottom roughness, the model results underestimated tide in the estuary. The modeled salinity concentration should be very sensitive to the change of roughness in the James and Chickahominy Rivers. The salinity in the Chickahominy River could decrease by a maximum of 2 ppt if roughness is increased to 0.4 cm. The model is more sensitive to bottom roughness where the water depth is shallow.

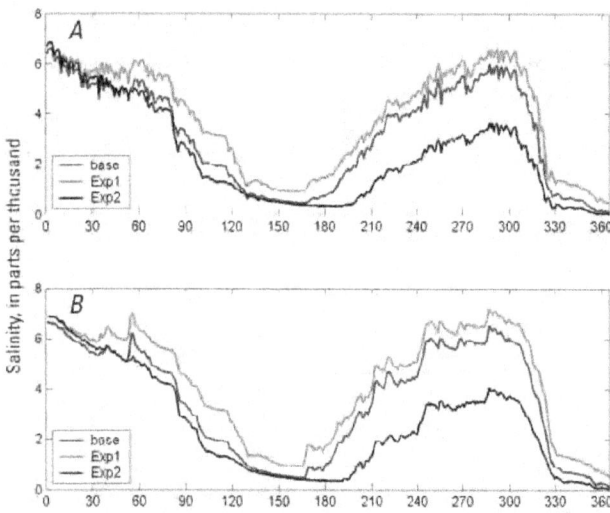

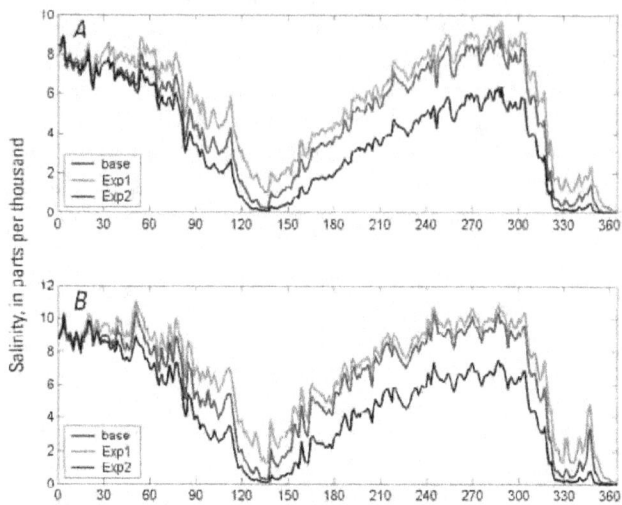

Figure 1-6A.   Comparison of model results between Base Case, Test 1 (decrease river discharge by 20 percent), and Test 2 (decrease salinity concentration at the open boundary by 15 percent) at the Chickahominy station; *A*, surface, *B*, bottom.

Figure 1-6C.   Comparison of model results between Base Case, Test 1 (decrease river discharge by 20 percent), and Test 2 (decrease salinity concentration at the open boundary by 15 percent) at the RET5.2 station; *A*, surface, *B*, bottom.

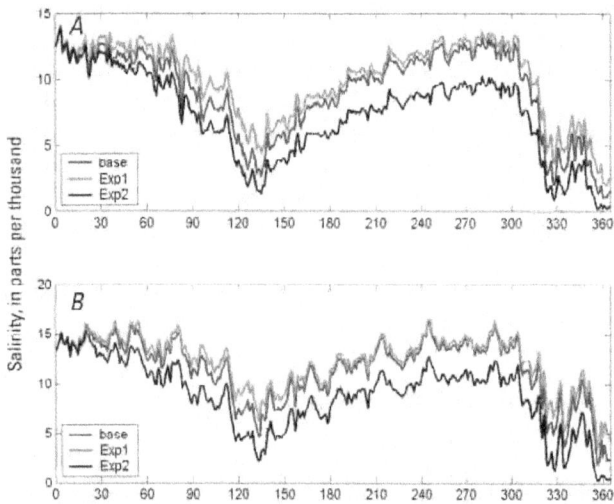

Figure 1-6B.   Comparison of model results between Base Case, Test 1 (decrease river discharge by 20 percent), and Test 2 (decrease salinity concentration at the open boundary by 15 percent) at the LE5.1 station; *A*, surface, *B*, bottom.

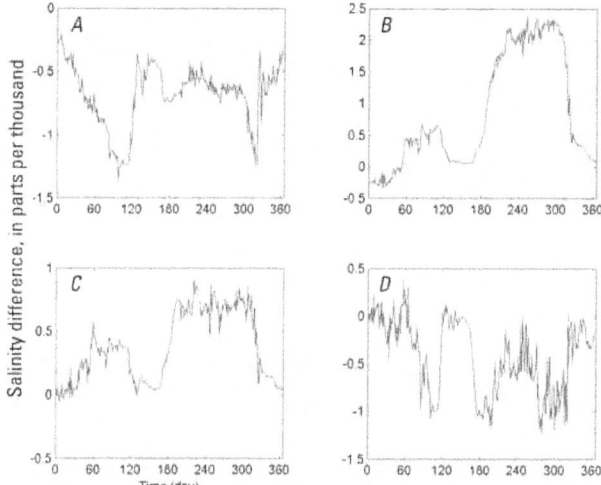

Figure 1-7A. Time series of salinity differences between the Base Case and model sensitivity Tests 1 through 4 at the Chickahominy station at the surface; *A*, Test 1, *B*, Test 2, *C*, Test 3, and *D*, Test 4.

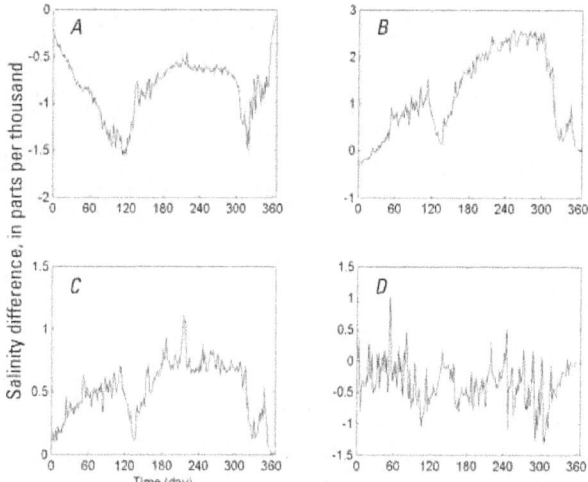

Figure 1-7C. Time series of salinity differences between the Base Case and model sensitivity Tests 1 through 4 at the RET5.2 station at the surface; *A*, Test 1, *B*, Test 2, *C*, Test 3, and *D*, Test 4.

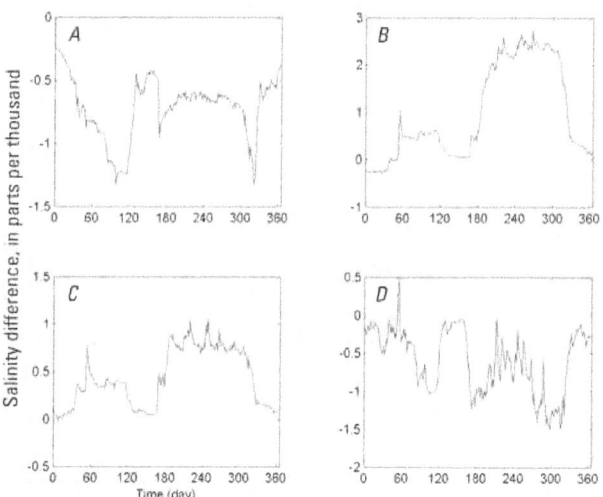

Figure 1-7B. Time series of salinity differences between the Base Case and model sensitivity Tests 1 through 4 at the Chickahominy station at the bottom; *A*, Test 1, *B*, Test 2, *C*, Test 3, and *D*, Test 4.

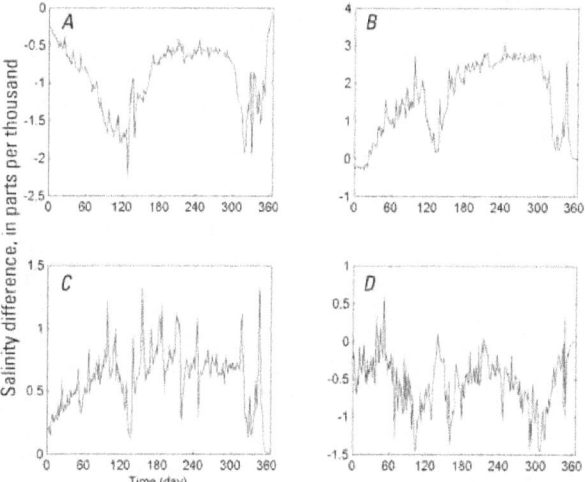

Figure 1-7D. Time series of salinity difference between Base Case and model sensitivity Tests 1 through 4 at the RET5.2 station at the bottom; *A*, Test 1, *B*, Test 2, *C*, Test 3, and *D*, Test 4.

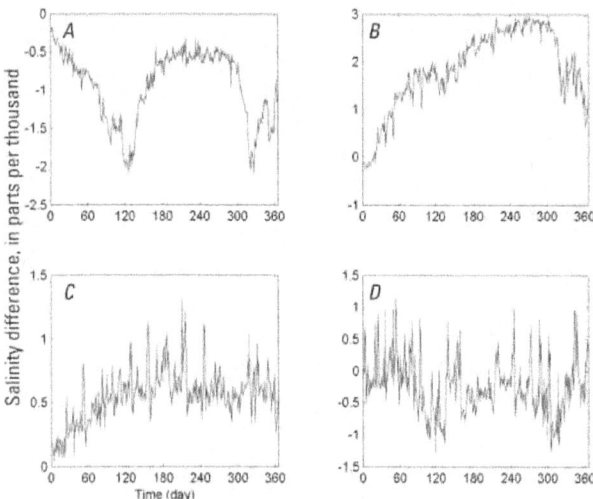

Figure 1-7E. Time series of salinity differences between the Base Case and model sensitivity Tests 1 through 4 at the LE5.1 station at the surface; *A*, Test 1, *B*, Test 2, *C*, Test 3, and *D*, Test 4.

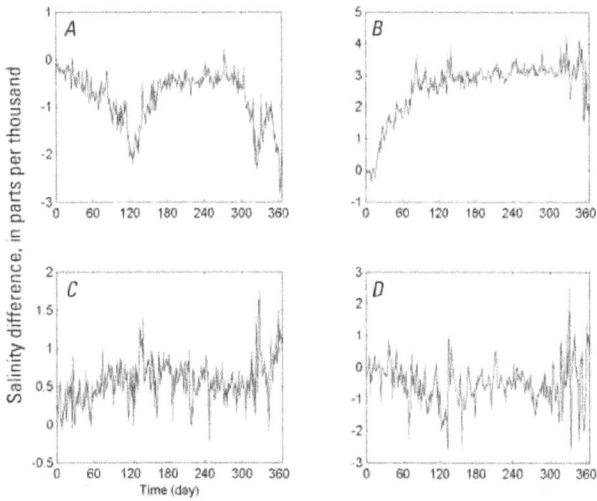

Figure 1-7F. Time series of salinity differences between the Base Case and model sensitivity Tests 1 through 4 at the LE5.1 station at the bottom; *A*, Test 1, *B*, Test 2, *C*, Test 3, and *D*, Test 4.

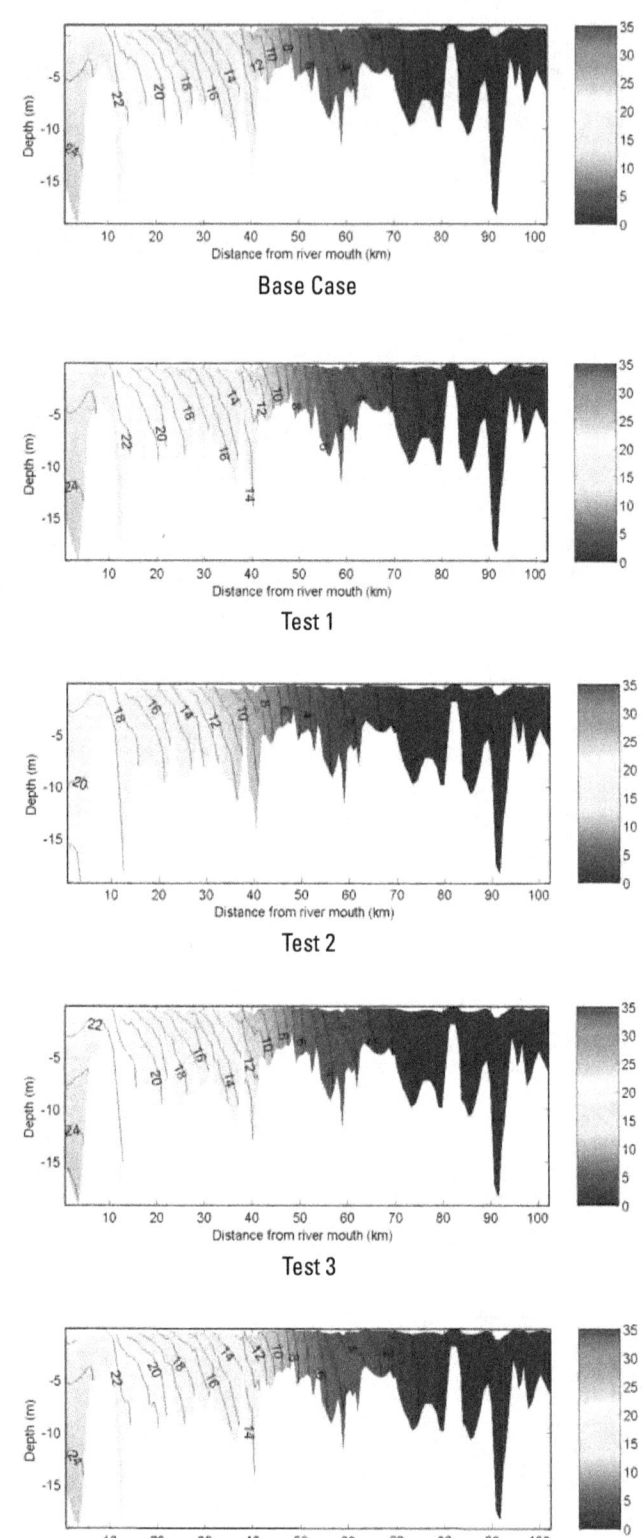

Base Case

Test 1

Test 2

Test 3

Test 4

Figure 1-8. James River mean salinity distribution (June and July) for the Base Case and sensitivity Tests 1 through 4. Salinity units (right axis) in parts per thousand.

Sensitivity to Wind Forcing (Test 4)

Wind acting on the surface generates vertical mixing near the surface, particularly for an upstream wind. In contrast, a downstream wind can increase estuarine circulation. Gong and others (2009) show that wind reduces estuarine circulation, thus reducing salinity intrusion. Results of Test 4 indicate that salinity intruded farther upstream because of the increase of estuarine circulation without wind (fig. 1-9). Salinity increased in both the tributary and the main channel of the James River.

The difference was up to 3 ppt in the Chickahominy River and more than 5 ppt in the James River.

The model sensitivity tests indicated that the numerical model performance highly depends on the model calibration and forcings used to drive the model. Large uncertainties are involved in these forcing data as a result of missing data, insufficient spatial coverage, and omission of local freshwater discharge, therefore discrepancies between model results and actual observations should be expected.

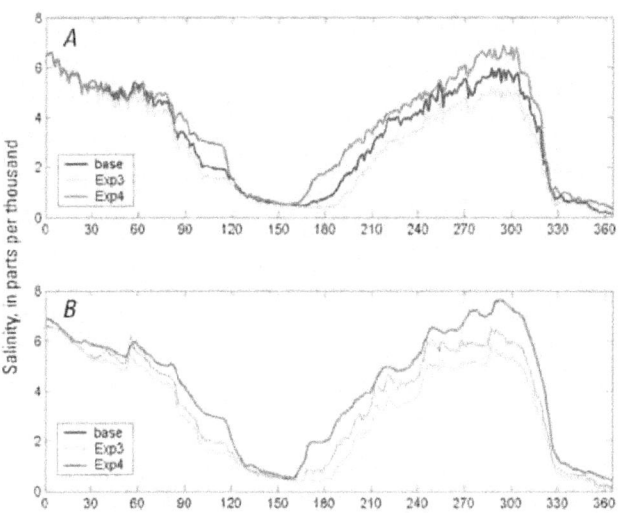

Figure 1-9A. Comparison of model results between the Base Case, Test 3 (doubling of the bottom roughness value), and Test 4 (turning off wind forcing at surface) at the Chickahominy station; *A*, surface, *B*, bottom.

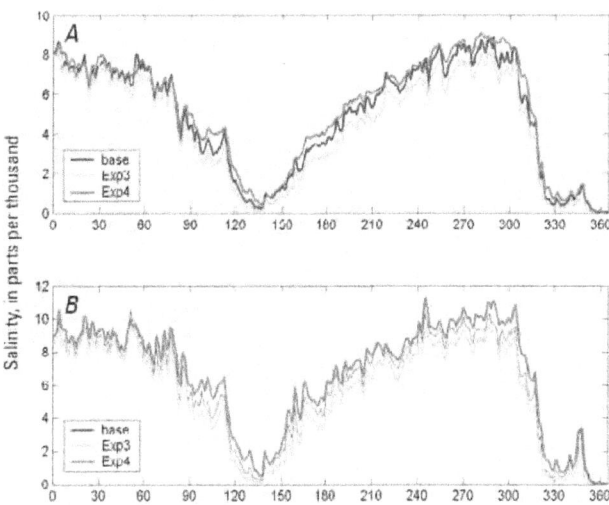

Figure 1-9C. Comparison of model results between the Base Case, Test 3 (doubling of the bottom roughness), and Test 4 (turning off wind forcing at surface) at the LE5.2 station; *A*, surface, *B*, bottom.

Figure 1-9B. Comparison of model results between the Base Case, Test 3 (doubling of the bottom roughness value), and Test 4 (turning off wind forcing at surface) at the RET5.1 station; *A*, surface, *B*, bottom.

For additional information regarding this publication, contact:

Director
USGS Virginia Water Science Center
1730 East Parham Road
Richmond, VA 23228
(804) 261-2600
email: dc_va@usgs.gov

Or visit the USGS Virginia Water Science Center Web site at:
http://va.water.usgs.gov

Prepared by:
USGS Science Publishing Network
Raleigh Publishing Service Center
3916 Sunset Ridge Road
Raleigh, NC 27607

www.ingramcontent.com/pod-product-compliance
Lightning Source LLC
Chambersburg PA
CBHW080352290526
45791CB00009BA/2840